Larry

Larry

A Biography

Donald J. Norton

of Lawrence D. Bell

Nelson-Hall nh Chicago

LIBRARY OF CONGRESS CATALOGING IN PUBLICATION DATA

Norton, Donald J
  Larry, a biography of Lawrence D. Bell.

  Bibliography: p.
  Includes index.
  1. Bell, Lawrence Dale, 1894–1956.   2. Aircraft
industry—United States—Biography. I.   Title.
TL540.B395N67   338.7′62913′00924 [B]   80-27791
ISBN 0-88229-615-9

Manufactured in the United States of America

10 9 8 7 6 5 4 3 2 1

To Jean

Contents

Young Bell drops out of school and follows his older brother into the exhibition flying business. He becomes a mechanic for the team, which included famed stunt man Lincoln Beachey; but the partnership ends on July 4, 1913, when a crash takes his brother's life.

Broken-hearted, Larry quits aviation; but a pontoon-building job with an out-of-work friend draws him back, and he goes to work for the Glenn L. Martin Co. The young company builds the bomber used by Pancho Villa in combat a year before World War I.

Martin moves to Cleveland and, as World War I ends, builds the first twin-engine U.S. bomber. General Billy Mitchell uses this airplane to stun his superiors with the realization that battleships are vulnerable to aerial attack.

Foreword

I am delighted that Donald J. Norton has written a definitive biography of my admired friend Lawrence D. (Larry) Bell. Larry, through the years, made great contributions to aviation and has never received proper credit for his effective efforts.

He saw his first airplane in 1910—the same year that I did—and was an aviation enthusiast ever since. That enthusiasm, a fine mind, and a skillful hand combined to provide the successes enumerated in the present volume. First as a "grease monkey" for his brother Grover Bell and Lincoln Beachey and later as the designer and builder of outstanding aircraft.

When Larry first became interested in aviation, airplanes had a top speed of around 40 miles per hour and a ceiling of about 4,000 feet. At the time of his death in 1956, his supersonic X-2 had just been flown at a speed of 2,148 miles per hour and to an altitude of 126,200 feet. The technology was at hand to put man into earth orbit and, with further development, on the moon.

Larry, whom I was proud to have as a personal friend, was dedicated to excellence. This and his vision made him one of the outstanding individuals of his era.

J. H. Doolittle
Los Angeles, California

Larry Bell had a sense of history that was just as strong as his ability to see the trends that aviation and aerospace would take in the future. Several times during the XS-1 program, I was his guest in Buffalo. He would proudly show me memorabilia he had collected in his long career. He never seemed to throw anything away that had to do with aviation and his company.

When Larry died in 1956, these precious things were shipped, as requested in his will, to his home town, Mentone, Indiana. With a population of about eight hundred, the good people of this community were in no position to set up a proper display, so the collection was carefully stored. And today, Mentone has started a major fund-raising effort to build the Lawrence D. Bell Aircraft Museum. I was very proud to help kick off that effort. I know they will be successful.

The museum and this book give Larry his rightful place in American history. Knowing him personally was an inspiration for me, and I am sure his story will be an inspiration for America's young pioneers of the future.

Charles E. Yeager
Cedar Ridge, California

Preface

Until now, the Larry Bell story has been untold. Bell was a high school dropout who gained international prominence as a builder of helicopters and high speed aircraft, yet he refused to stand still long enough for a biographer to get him on paper.

When Larry died in 1956, it looked as though he had taken his story with him. He left only some press releases, a clipping file, cartons of papers generated year-by-year as head of a company, and a few hours of taped reminiscences. But spread out from coast to coast were the men and women Bell had known and influenced. Often referred to as "the Bell family," they remember the man vividly. Much of this book is based on interviews with members of this "family."

Bell had the kind of charm that could give an auditorium full of people the feeling that he was talking to each one of them personally. One man who said he knew Larry Bell was asked how he had gotten to know him. "I heard him speak at the Statler Hotel in 1940," he said.

A man of contrasts, Bell loved airplanes but feared flying. He was a gregarious man but somehow remained a loner. He loved children but never had any of his own and never adopted any. And he was an important part of the creative process that produced his company's most advanced flying machines, yet he was not an engineer.

Bell's story is part technical, part inspirational. Not long after Bell fought to get his new company started, he was battling to meet World War production demands. Then came a postwar proxy fight. After that came the bloody strike of 1949, when once again it looked like the man might lose the company he loved.

This book is for American history buffs as much as it is for the aviation history audience. Told for the first time is the story of Bell's spy trip to Nazi Germany in 1938, which Larry disguised as a casual visit of an industrialist interested in German aviation developments. At his farewell dinner, a German general told Larry he was free to tell what he saw but added, "Please, Herr Bell, one thing—do not tell the British!"

Here is the story of the huge Bell bomber plant at Marietta, Georgia. Staffed by rural workers, this project started the southward flow of industry that has continued ever since. And there are the stories of the XP-59A, America's first jet, the XS-1 first supersonic airplane, and the Bell helicopters.

Here is Larry Bell's story, a chapter in the history of American aviation.

Acknowledgments

Many good people share in the making of this book. Closest to the project was Dorothy Ray, who typed and retyped the manuscript very professionally over a period of two years.

The management of Bell Aerospace Textron provided access to the Larry Bell papers and company records for the period 1935–56. Bell's top executives, William G. Gisel and Norton C. Willcox, also made it possible for me to be present at the Larry Bell enshrinement in the American Aviation Hall of Fame, and Constance Kastelowitz helped immensely with suggestions and with the financial side of the early company days by steering me to veteran attorney Mason Damon.

Ray and Pauline Whitman made available their files and memorabilia, and reviewed the complete original draft in 1976.

Robert M. Stanley reviewed the P-59 chapter and confirmed the hacksaw story told to me by Emmett McMahon. Stanley wrote that "the legend of my hacksaw exploits was related to an oversized rudder resulting in the airplane being directionally stiff, requiring lots of force to move the rudder at high speed." Stanley also noted: "I have to assume that you were not around during the time in question and suspect that you had a lot of fun researching the background whereby you write."

Francis W. Dunn's personal recollections were a priceless contribution, and his comments on the manuscript helped make it a more accurate reflection of Larry's life.

David G. Forman and Edward K. Paul were the sources for many of the best anecdotes, and Irma Brooks, Larry's housekeeper, very graciously provided a wealth of information on Larry's life away from the plant.

Julie Scheffler combed the Bell files and found many of the best historical photographs.

Bart Kelley and Floyd Carlson helped with the helicopter chapter, and Tex Johnston—still flying and living in Melbourne, Florida—assisted with the test pilot side of the story.

Other Bell people who helped are: Ed Marek, Mark O'Connell, Mickey McCarthy, Bill Fuller, Joe Bellonte, Milly George, Earl Stanton, Stan Turner, Ed Rhoades, Steve Gaspar, Irene Hoague, Dick McKee, Mary Margaret Woolams, Stu Watt, Chuck Kreiner, Barbara Meholick, Clare Orndorff, Eleanor Ponto, John Colt, Scott Hammon, Robert Sherwood, Albert Spindler, Walt MacMurray, Joe Cannon, Don Conlin, Walter Adams, Elsa Spitznagel, Nick Insana, Stan Smith, John Marmion, Herb Sommer, Harry Cleveland, Dorothy Cursons, Marge Ludascher, Gene Schneider, Tom Lennon, Bob Roach, Charley Haymes, Dave Marshall, Ed Delaney, Bill Johnson, and John Weisbeck.

Thanks also to Dominic Pisa at the Smithsonian Institution's Air and Space Museum; H. S. Gann at Douglas Aircraft Co.; Linda Haering at the *Petaluma Argus-Courier*; Ms. Nuneman at Santa Monica High School; Valerie Petta at Martin Marietta Corp.; Lindbergh biographer Leonard Mosley; Jim Tuttle at Rockwell International; J. F. Isabel at General Dynamics; A. V. Krochalis at the Naval Intelligence Command; Robert Casari of the American Aviation Historical Society; Klaus Peters at Messerschmitt-Bolkow-Blohm; Charles A. Brady of Canisius College; Bob Watson and Ed Kelly at the *Buffalo Evening News*; Len Feldmann and Len Delmar at the *Buffalo Courier-Express*; Bob Whetstone and R"J" Hill in Mentone and Alvin Rockhill in Warsaw, Ind.; Jean Ross Howard at the Aerospace Industries Association; Mel Zisfein at the Smithsonian; and Harry Kolcum at *Aviation Week & Space Technology*.

Inspiration was provided by Lawrence Dale Bell Norton, who arrived on Flag Day in 1976.

1

Tragedy
at the Start

The stocky young man leaned forward and nudged the venerable mare with his knees. He saw opportunity ahead. A group of men were digging where they shouldn't and Larry Bell knew it. "What're you looking for down there, Mr. Middlecoff?"

"Supposed to be a shutoff valve here someplace," said a heavy, dark-haired man, wiping his brow with his sleeve.

"Say, you're way off," said Larry. "The only valve around here is a couple hundred feet this way."

They followed him until Bell slid off his horse, took one of the shovels, and uncovered the valve. Sixteen-year-old Larry Bell was a familiar figure in Jacob Middlecoff's Santa Monica hardware store. He had asked for work but had been turned down by a man who had two sons already working in the store.

The next time Larry walked in the store, he was offered a part-time job as clerk. Bell was busy at school as well as at home, where he was installing wiring for his parents, but there was no hesitation. Middlecoff offered wages. It was 1910, and Larry Bell had his first paying job.

"If you're interested in a career, there's nothing more down to earth than the hardware business," said Middlecoff.

"That's my ambition!" replied Bell.

Larry was a sophomore in Santa Monica's Polytechnic High School, where his chief interests were mechanics and woodworking. After school, he quickly learned the hardware business. In a short time, experienced plumbers and electricians sought him out because he talked their language.

1

Nights, at home, Larry installed gas, electric, and water pipes. The Bells and their friends held a small celebration when the job was done—and for good reason: for the first time in their long lives, Mr. and Mrs. Bell lived in a house with indoor plumbing!

Lawrence Dale Bell was born on April 5, 1894, in Mentone, Indiana (population 400), the youngest of ten children of Isaac Evans Bell and Harriet Sarber Bell. The Bell ancestors had slowly drifted west since their forebears had arrived from Scotland, Germany, and Ireland, more than one hundred years before. Isaac Bell, who operated a small lumber mill, had moved to Mentone from Knox County, Ohio, after his parents had brought him to Ohio from the Pennsylvania Dutch country. He often showed visitors a newspaper clipping about his Irish grandfather, William Moore, which told how Moore had built the first cabin on Lake Erie, where Cleveland, Ohio, is now located.

Harriet Bell (whose mother was a Lee from Virginia and believed to be a distant relative of Robert E. Lee) was a school teacher who was ambitious for her children. She spent many hours with them in the kitchen near the warmth of the wood stove, reading and testing their minds. As each child came of age, it was Mrs. Bell who urged them to leave Mentone and find a life where greater opportunity existed. Several children moved to California, married, and raised families.

In 1907, when Larry was the only child still living with them, Isaac and Harriet decided to close the lumber business and retire to California to be near their children. Two sons, Will and Grover, had already selected a house for them in Santa Monica. Also living nearby was a daughter, Mary Legardia (Gardie), and another son, Vaughn.

Will managed a waterworks and arranged a part-time job for his father. The parents purchased a home at 2402 16th Street, three lots away from Will's house. Everything was ready for Mr. and Mrs. Bell when they stepped aboard the train in Warsaw, Indiana, for the long trip west. Larry had never traveled before, and the trip was a matter of great excitement.

"Me!" he exclaimed, "On the Southern Pacific!"

The family traveled day and night, sitting on the reed seats of a tourist coach. They had a huge wicker basket filled with food prepared by friends and neighbors. At stops, Larry was sent running for coffee.

Larry saw his first streetcars as the train arrived in Chicago. When the conductor came through announcing a twenty-minute stop, Larry grabbed the coffee bucket and headed down the street to find a restaurant.

He was back in ten minutes. The train was gone, but why panic? Train movements during stops were not uncommon, so he sat on a bench and waited for it to come back. After a few minutes he asked a stationman when it would return.

"Boy, that train's not coming back," said the man. "It's just now leaving Union Station, downtown."

"Can you tell me how to get there?"

Still carrying the bucket, Larry ran four blocks to a streetcar stop and described his plight to the conductor of the first car to come along. Before Larry had finished, the man said "hold on." The streetcar passed every stop for several blocks and dropped Bell at the railroad station. Larry shouted thanks on his way out the door. As he neared the gate, a formidable gateman stood in the way. Larry once again told his story, but this time it didn't work.

Then he spotted his father talking to a railroad official, and his reaction was instantaneous—Larry dropped the coffee, ducked, and ran between the gateman's legs. "Father," he shouted, running up to his father. "I'm here!"

Years later, Bell summed up the experience: "I had no money, no experience, no anything. All I had was a bucket of coffee that was gettin' colder every minute."

Larry heard talk of the wonders of aviation as he wandered the train on that long railroad trip. He was curious; but it wasn't until three years later, when the nation's first major air show was held at Dominquez Field near Long Beach, that he actually saw an airplane. With brothers Vaughn and Grover, and Grover's fiancee, Margaret Kent, Larry went to see the show.

Several of aviation's biggest names were in the competition. Of the two dozen licensed U.S. pilots, Dominquez had attracted Glenn H. Curtiss, Charles F. Willard, Charles K. Hamilton, and Louis Palhan, as well as Balloonists Roy Knabenshue and Lincoln Beachey. In ten days of competition, Palhan set a distance mark of 45 miles and an altitude record of 4,146 feet, and Curtiss made a passenger-and-pilot speed record of 55 miles per hour. Beachey, an aerial showman famed for spectacular balloon and dirigible flights, beat Knabenshue in a race around the track—two bumbling airships moving at a few miles per

*Larry, at about age twelve months, poses in a
photo studio*

*Isaac and Harriet Bell with some of their children in
Mentone, about 1870.*

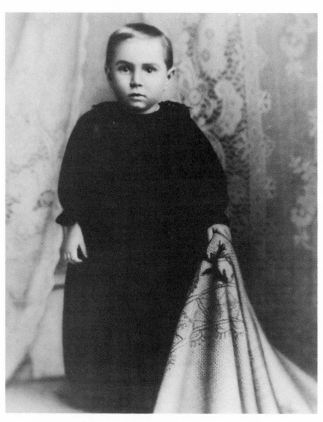

Baby Bell in a Warsaw, Indiana, photo studio.

Larry's portrait just as he was becoming an adolescent.

In this home in Mentone, Indiana, Isaac and Harriet Bell raised ten children.

hour in the same general direction, wildly cheered by the crowd below. But Beachey's days as a balloonist were near an end. He was fascinated by the performances of Palhan, Curtiss, and the heavier-than-air machines and decided to leave balloons for airplanes.

Dominquez was a glorious confusion of men, aircraft, the drone of engines, and the scent of gasoline, oil, and sweat. Vaughn, six years older than Larry, was driver for the trip home. The car broke down eighteen times, giving the young passengers plenty of time to talk about what they had seen. Without realizing it, they were being drawn by the pioneering fascination that permeated the early days of flying. A pilot, Miss Gertrude Bacon, once described the feeling in *The Aeroplane: An Historical Survey:*

"Picture, if you can, what it meant for the first time: When all the world of aviation was young and fresh and untried; when to rise at all was a glorious adventure, and to find oneself flying swiftly in the air, the too-good-to-be-true realization of a life-long dream. You wonderful aerial record-breakers of today and of the years to come, whose exploits I may only marvel at and envy, I have experienced something that can never be yours and can never be taken away from me—the rapture, the glory, and the glamour of the 'very beginning.'"

At home, the Bell boys went to work on model planes that resembled box kites. Altitude depended on the pull-string's length. Speed was a matter of leg power. But certain design features from real planes were included, depending upon what the boys had thought significant at Dominquez; and the boys made some improvements of their own.

Larry was still in high school, but Grover was a grown man of twenty-seven who quickly became bored with model airplanes. He decided to try a career in aviation and looked up the Glenn L. Martin Company in the Los Angeles telephone directory. (The leading local airplane manufacturer could be found listed under Amusements!) Martin himself taught Bell to fly. The price was steep—$500, but it led to immediate renown for Grover. He was the first pilot to land in Santa Monica; and, to the great satisfaction of Larry, this historic landing was made on open lots next to the Bell homes on 16th Street.

Grover went to work for Martin as exhibition flyer and instructor. In 1912, he sold some property, bought an old Martin biplane for about $2,500, and went on the road with Lincoln Beachey while continuing to work for Martin.

A flier with his own airplane could easily make a living in 1912, and Grover had teamed with some of the most talented associates of the time. By 1912, Lincoln Beachey was building a reputation as the greatest of all exhibition pilots. Glenn Martin not only built airplanes, but was also one of the country's best pilots.

When business was slow at Middlecoff's, Larry would pull a wad of newspaper clippings and read of the exploits of Beachey, Martin, and Bell. Two things happened that year: Larry completed his studies at Santa Monica Polytechnic (but dropped out before graduation day), and Middlecoff offered him a job as store manager. The time for a decision had come. "Thanks, Mr. Middlecoff," said Larry, "but I've decided to go into aviation with my brother and Mr. Beachey."

He started as a grease monkey, traveling with the team and living day and night in repair shops, tents, hangars, and open fields, wherever the airplanes were.

Aviation was a special fraternity in 1912. The men and women had no interest other than aircraft and the progress they were making with them. The business world ignored airplanes, and there was little government money in aviation. It was almost completely sustained by the flying fraternity. Planes, parts, engines, and technology changed hands like merchandise at a trading post.

Grover Evans Bell became a well known aviator on the West Coast. He received license No. 201 Federation Aeronautique International in late 1912 from H. LaVern Twining of the Aero Club of California. Flying home to Santa Monica that Christmas Day proved his skill. The *Los Angeles Tribune and Express* reported: "His journey yesterday was a perilous one. He crossed Mt. Hollywood at an altitude of 2,500 feet. He lost his way in the fog and was forced to descend 1,000 feet while over Pico Heights and make three circles. If it is foggy tomorrow he will not fly back [to Griffith Aviation Park in Los Angeles]."

Typical of the exhibitions at the time was a flight Grover made for Commonwealth Home Builders Company in Los Angeles. They were selling a development known as Gotham Park, near Manchester Avenue, and advertised that Grover would make "a grand cross country exhibition flight" from Santa Monica to drop "money orders" on the crowd below. Each money order was good for a payment on a Gotham Park lot: Tours available. The promotion produced $42,500 in lot sales.

Grover mastered all the known flying techniques, and Larry was a source of boundless energy and enthusiasm. The young men had become important members of the Martin Company, which had expanded to occupy two floors at 943 South Los Angeles Street—a vast improvement from the first Martin plant, the abandoned Methodist Church in Santa Ana where Martin had built his first airplane in 1909. A Los Angeles newspaper reported:

"Bell [flying a biplane once used by Blanch Stuart Scott] has a larger motor in his engine [sic] now. He purchased the 'Copper Kettle,' a 60 horse-power Hall-Scott. It was one of the first motors turned out by that factory. After being in use around San Francisco for some time, it went South. Didier Masson used it for a number of flights. A. V. Hartle, the aviator who was killed at Dominquez Field, used it. Glenn Martin used it part of the time at Chicago and on his return to this city sold it to Bell."

Never, except in sports writing, would the public be so completely informed of the progress of men and women training to be weekend heroes.

Aviation interest was not entirely civilian. An army lieutenant named Henry Harley Arnold pulled an aerial hoax over Washington, D.C., on July 10, 1911, when the city anxiously awaited the arrival of long-distance flier Harry Atwood, a Bostonian who was making a highly publicized 461 mile flight to the capitol.

Congress was in session, so page boys were assigned to keep their eyes on the sky. Every so often, someone would issue the cry, "Here he comes! Atwood is here!" and everyone—including Vice President James S. Sherman—would run out to take a look. Finally, a speck appeared in the sky. Then they heard the engine. The crowd, which grew to fifty thousand, wildly cheered. The airplane circled buildings, roared down the wide streets, and put on a thrilling performance. But it did not land and soon was gone.

A day later it was learned what happened. Atwood had been grounded by mechanical problems near Arnold's flying field, and the young army officer had seen an opportunity for a hoax. Fun-loving "Hap" Arnold would become a five-star general in World War II, but Harry Atwood ended up the hero of 1911. When he finally arrived in Washington, Atwood was greeted by thousands, and President Taft shook his hand.

There is a distinction between the exhibition flying of the early

1900s and the barnstorming after World War I. The exhibitionists were pioneering idealists who advanced the technology of
flying and paid the bills by putting on an exciting show. Barn-
stormers were jobless military pilots who made a living by stunt-
ing with war surplus machines.

Before World War I, the world closely watched the aviation
death toll: One killed in 1908, 4 in 1909, 33 in 1910, 73 in 1911,
and 111 in 1912. Grover's new bride, Margaret Kent Bell, worried and prayed. Her headstrong husband was traveling, flying,
and making headlines. Grover had dreams of greater things in
the future, when he, Margaret, and Larry traveled by train to
Petaluma, California, for a July 4, 1913, exhibition flight.

Upon arrival, the flying team visited Kenilworth Park, a half-
mile racetrack where the holiday crowd would gather. After
greeting the Independence Day committee, Larry and Grover
assembled the aircraft and made some noisy engine run-ups.
The takeoffs, landings, and stunts could safely take place directly in front of the grandstand. The only problem was tall
trees. The park was surrounded with them, and Grover would
have to fly in and out through one opening.

Glenn Martin's May 31 agreement with J. E. Olmsted, chairman of the Petaluma Aviation Committee, had promoted Grover
as "a very careful and clever operator and you may rest assured
that you will receive some very fine flying of a high grade. Mr.
Bell made some very daring and notable flights last year and
has acted in the capacity of chief instructor in our school during
the winter. Mr. Bell will add dignity to the occasion, being a
thorough gentleman in every respect and like other aviators
who became famous, never drinks a drop."

Martin added $50 to the contract because the community
could not provide an airplane hangar, and the deal was closed
at $750. The performance was to be free to the public.

Grover and Larry were celebrities. The *Petaluma* (California)
Argus reported that "the flight will be by far the best ever given
in the county," and casually noted that Grover "will probably
fly over the city . . . so keep your eyes on the air for the next
few days."

On the morning of July 4, Grover checked his airplane with a
brief test flight and was bringing it through the opening in the
trees for the landing. Suddenly he was in mortal danger.

"There were six race horses tied up to a post," Larry recalled. "They got scared and broke loose, running down the

Isaac and Harriet Bell, Santa Monica, Calif., 1914.

The Bell boys' first model airplane, 1910. Larry is kneeling at left. Grover is smoking a cigar at right.

Larry, Grover's girlfriend Margaret Kent, and Grover at the Dominquez aviation meet, 1910.

A lifetime lover of animals and children, Larry frolics with a calf and a dog at his parents' home, 1914.

Larry Bell, second from left, at Griffith Aviation Park in 1913.

Larry in the seat of his brother's airplane at Griffith Air Park, Los Angeles, 1912.
The man at the propeller is Charles Day.

Larry poses in Grover's biplane on a Sunday afternoon in 1912.

One of the last pictures taken of Grover Bell before his fatal crash on July 4, 1913. The aircraft is Grover's personal plane, believed to be a Curtiss 1911 Model D.

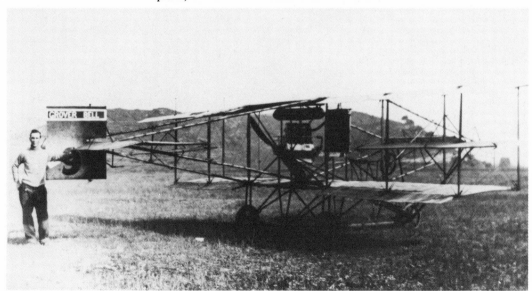

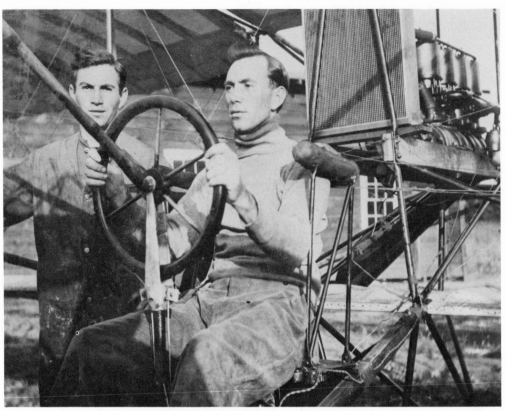

The Bell Exhibition Flying Team.

One of Larry's favorite pictures of Grover.

Grover taxies on pontoons built by his grease monkey brother, Larry Bell.

field in front of Grover's airplane. The only way he could avoid landing on the horses and hurting or killing them was to try to make—at very low altitude, nearly on the ground—a 180-degree turn and go out the only opening there was. The airplane couldn't complete the turn. He missed the horses but dragged a wing and crashed."

On July 5, the *Argus* reported:

"Grover E. Bell, the skilled aviator who was to have made three flights at Kenilworth Park as the stellar attraction of the big celebration in this city, is lying probably fatally injured at the local hospital, the result of an unfortunate accident as he was landing at 8:30 on Friday morning after a trial flight. . . .

"While it has been stated that he was injured while trying to dodge a band of horses in the field on alighting, many of the citizens who were watching the flights with field glasses, say that while in mid air, he appeared to be in distress just before the descent. A sudden spurt of blue smoke was emitted from the engine and auto owners who watched, say that it appeared as if his engine had flooded.

"He descended very rapidly, his flight being watched by hundreds of people from the hill section of the city, and several at the grounds. He has not been able to tell the tale, but in his delirium after the accident, repeatedly called 'shut her off, shut her off!' Bell's wife and brother were immediately at his side, Mrs. Bell showing wonderful nerve for a while. . . .

"After several hours the sufferer became conscious, but at seven o'clock on Friday evening again lapsed into unconsciousness and since that time has been in a comatose condition. His wife and brother are at the bedside."

Grover died that day.

2

Pancho Villa's
Air Force

The Bell brothers had planned a company of their own to build a new line of airplanes. There had been long discussions about the possibilities of rotary-wing and amphibious aircraft. Grover would earn start-up money by doing exhibition flying, and Larry was to set up the shop. But, as Larry crated the broken pieces of Grover's airplane, there were no more dreams. He wanted no more of aviation.

"I decided I would do something else. I didn't do anything for a couple of months," Larry recalled.

In August, he received a wire from the aviation committee in Petaluma: "In pursuance of a resolution authorizing us to do so, [we] herewith present to you the sum of Four Hundred and Thirty-Eight ($438) Dollars. The said amount is a donation by the citizens of Petaluma to assist in defraying the expenses of the last illness of your dear relative, and our esteemed friend, Grover E. Bell. . . ."

Larry sent a note of thanks, but it was painful even to think of Petaluma. He might never have returned to aviation if it hadn't been for the persistence of a close family friend, Dave Hunt, who needed help getting a job.

"You're one of the few people who've built airplane floats," Hunt told Bell as they drove to the airplane shop of Jay Gage. "Would you just show me how and let me do the work?"

At the shop, Gage assured them the job was theirs if they worked as a team. "But it's got to be right," Gage told them. "Two wing floats and the center float—like the ones you've made, Larry."

Bell, who had become a chain-smoker, stared silently out the window as they drove home. Hunt began talking. He had lost his job as a car salesman because he had taken several days off to stay with the Bell family during Grover's wake. "There's no question that I'll help you," Larry said.

They went to work around the clock. It was like old times. They slept in the shop, cooked over blow-torches, and had beautifully crafted wooden floats finished in a week. Working with his hands again had cleared Larry's mind, and he accepted a job at the Glenn L. Martin Company as a nine-dollar-a-week stockroom clerk.

Martin was tall, scholarly looking, and aloof. He was all business, relying heavily on the judgment of his mother, who was frequently in his office. And he was a first-rate flier, one of the best exhibitionists in the country. When it was necessary, Martin met the thirty-employee payroll of his plant at 943 South Los Angeles Street by working weekends as a daredevil.

Martin had a flair for the bizarre. He wore a skull-hugging dark leather helmet that left only a small oval for his somber face. The costume became his trademark: The Flying Dude. In addition to stunts, Martin was a specialist in sales promotion flying that required exact timing.

Just before Christmas, 1913, he took a young woman named Tiny Broadwick aloft in a promotion for downtown merchants. Miss Broadwick looked seductive and demure as she tossed gift certificates to the crowd below. She also threw out bundles of a miniature edition of the *Los Angeles Tribune and Express*, "first ever published exclusively for aerial distribution," the paper claimed.

Despite these circus-style performances, Martin's relationships with his work force and even his customers were stiff and formal. "He did not know how to talk to people," Larry said. Throughout their close relationship over the years, Martin never called Larry by any other name than "Bell." In contrast, Larry was a gregarious, friendly person. He wanted everyone to call him Larry, and almost everyone did. The only other exceptions were his brother Vaughn and sister Gardie, and his friends and relatives in Indiana, who referred to him as Lawrence.

Although Larry was not a pilot and rarely flew, he knew enough about flying to teach the basics to a young Japanese naval officer who walked into the plant late one afternoon. "I told him all the pilots were out of town on exhibitions," Bell said, "but he persisted. And he had the necessary $500 fee." Larry took an old biplane that was parked behind the plant, put a used engine in it, and made a certified flier of the man.

"I taught him by the jump-plane method," said Larry. "The aircraft was underpowered, so I told him to add power a little at a time until he'd finally get off the ground about a foot. He'd come back down again in about fifty feet and then jump off again. He'd keep doing that until he'd be flying the whole length of the field. Then he would make a circle, and it wasn't much longer before he had a license in his hand."

At a farewell dinner in the Jutland Hotel, the young Japanese ceremoniously gave Bell a fine wristwatch to show his gratitude. He never did find out he'd learned to fly from a nonpilot!

Bell had quickly won the admiration of Glenn Martin, because Larry was a total company man. He was an enthusiastic hard worker who never seemed to want to go home. Put in charge of the tool room, Larry solved a problem caused by workmen hiding or locking their tools in out-of-the-way places. No one could find the right tool when the owner wasn't around. Bell, the future super-salesman, was able to persuade these rough, suspicious men to trust him with their tools, ending production tie-ups and frenzied searches for needed equipment.

Rather than sit idle in the toolroom during lulls, Larry volunteered to build shipping crates. "Just leave the wood outside," Larry told Martin. "I can build crates in my spare time."

It wasn't long before Larry was shop foreman, and his ideas and influence continued to spread. Larry designed what would become a well-known Martin emblem, a star against a blue disk surrounded by a red circle. (By coincidence, the U.S. Army Air Corps later came up with a similar insignia. "The corps tried to get Martin to give it up," said Bell. "But he refused.")

Bell was unmarried and lived with Gardie and her husband at 1406 Fifth Ave. He rode a trolley to work, giving him time to plan to the last detail what was to become the most famous of all the Martin exhibitions: The Battle of the Clouds.

There had been experiments with aerial bombing. The first recorded tests had been made on June 30, 1911, when Glenn Curtiss dropped dummy bombs on the shape of a ship marked by buoys on Lake Keuka, New York. The first live bombs were dropped by a Wright aircraft that same year. But these experiments didn't have the kind of showmanship Larry had in mind.

After a routine business session with Martin, he introduced his idea. "We've got just enough cash to pull it off," said Larry. "The aircraft's ready to go. There's plenty of wood and fabric for the fort and the cannon. All we need to buy is black powder and dynamite, and maybe some oranges and grapefruit."

"Dynamite? Bell, you said dynamite?"

Larry explained that what he had in mind was a massive two-day show: A mock battlefield—complete with a fort, cannon, and soldiers—to stage something dramatic and new: bombing from the air.

The crowd paid one dollar a head to see "The Battle of the Clouds." Lincoln Beachey opened the show by performing his latest tricks—including a stunt in which he flew at ground level before the grandstand, dipped a wing, and scooped up a piece of cloth from the field.

Then Tiny Broadwick, who had become a regular part of the Martin Company exhibition team, did a parachute jump, and the veteran balloon man, Roy Knabenshue, went aloft in his giant bumbling contraption. Bell was in command on the ground while Martin took to the air. The cloth-and-wood fort was painted to look like stone. A long dummy cannon stood at the center, and two smaller mock guns aimed out of towers on each side. Martin employees, dressed in military costumes, were deployed here and there carrying rifles loaded with blank cartridges.

After a disorganized first show, Bell got things running smoothly the second day. He controlled a large panel of door-bell buttons that were connected by wires to a dozen pits dug at various places in front of the fort. In these pits, black powder was ignited electrically as Martin flew by, tossing oranges. (Since bombs in 1913 were something most commonly thought of as being round with a fuse sticking out one end, ripe California oranges seemed closest to the real thing.)

As Martin flew near, Larry pushed the proper buttons each time the aircraft "bombed" near one of the pits. Two things happened every time Bell pushed a button: First, the black powder in the pit ignited with a puff, blowing dirt high in the air. But the black powder, which was safe to use with men nearby, did not have much of a bang, so separate wires set off sticks of dynamite behind the fort.

The big cannon swung up into sight, let go a dummy charge, and then disappeared again. Each time it went down, crewmen placed a trail of black powder along a metal trough inside its canvas barrel. This led to a smoke charge at the muzzle, which puffed ferociously in the direction of the grandstand.

The aircraft was an easy winner. As it bombed, pieces of the fort went flying in every direction, kicked out by Larry's ground crew. There were cheers from the grandstand when especially large chunks tumbled to the ground.

The finale was a near disaster. The cannon caught fire, forcing crewmen to slap at it with blankets in an attempt to keep the entire fort from going up in smoke. Women screamed, the soldiers began to disappear in all directions, and the fort disappeared in a haze of smoke, flying dirt, and flaming canvas. Martin peered down coolly through his oval helmet, while Bell set off the last charges and ran from the scene of destruction. As the smoke cleared the stunned crowd sat silently for a moment before filing quietly out of the stands. Never had anything like it been seen before!

Juan and Pedro Alcaldez sat in the stands long after the show, talking intently, and later went out on the field to look at the debris. Then they went to the Martin shop. Glenn and Bell were counting the gate receipts they had carried away in a potato sack. They were onto something big, and they knew it. "Suppose we do the same show for the army?" Bell said. "How about building a battleship and inviting the navy to see it sink?"

"They're going to be knocking on the door," said Martin.

Then appeared the Alcaldez brothers. Pedro was squat and unsmiling, a sweaty man in a rumpled white suit. Juan was slender and elegantly dressed. He did the talking. "We are looking for an airplane to drop bombs," he told Martin and Bell. "Why?" asked Martin.

Juan showed credentials signed by the Mexican revolutionary, Francisco Pancho Villa—who at the time was in exile in the United States. Pancho was in Los Angeles when the newspapers announced "The Battle of the Clouds." Juan and Pedro were his emissaries.

"It looks like General Villa plans to go back into Mexico in style," said Larry, smiling.

The two Mexicans were expressionless. "What is the price of a bombing airplane and bombs?" asked Juan.

"Ten thousand dollars FOB Los Angeles for the airplane," said Martin. "Bombs are extra. We can give you delivery in two weeks. You will be responsible for shipment of the plane to Mexico."

Tiny Broadwick after her "Battle of the Clouds" parachute jump. The man at left is unidentified.

Glenn Martin with one of his early exhibition machines, probably a 1912 Curtiss Model E.

Martin and Larry Bell.

Lincoln Beachey's Martin tractor, about 1914.

Larry, businessman/backer Caleb Bragg, and Glenn Martin with a TT trainer in 1914.

The crew of "Battle of the Clouds" under the canvas cannon. Martin is second from right and Bell is third from left.

Action during "Battle of the Clouds."

Bell ready for a flight in a Martin trainer.

Juan nodded agreement, and Martin added: "We must have cash in advance."

"Open the suitcase," Juan told Pedro.

Neatly bundled inside was enough money for the entire project: bomber, bombs, shipping, and money to hire a pilot, Didier Masson, and a British mechanic named Tommy Dean. Pancho Villa was to have an air force.

Profits from "The Battle of the Clouds" and the Pancho Villa contract put Martin's company in the black. The shop quickly went to work modifying a two-seat tractor biplane so bombs could be stored within reach of the mechanic in the front seat. Bell personally designed and built bombs of two-and-a-half-inch iron pipe, two feet long. He filled these with dynamite and detonator caps that triggered the explosion on impact. After some trips to a nearby field for tests—dropping bombs by string-pull remote control—Bell balanced the pipe so it would detonate no matter which way it was tossed out of an airplane.

The world's first combat bomber was shipped by railway express to Tucson, Arizona. It was shunted south and assembled by its crew in a remote area of the desert, near the Mexican border. The next dawn, Masson and Dean flew it into Mexico to join troops headed by Villa and Venustiano Carranza. The aircraft went into action against various cities occupied by the federal forces of Villa's archenemy, General Victoriano Huerta, who had condemned Villa to death for insubordination a year earlier.

Huerta, alarmed, sent an urgent message to Washington. Press stories hinted that Glenn Martin's company might have been the manufacturer, and a reporter drove out to interview Martin. An airplane had been sold through the agency of Van M. Griffith to an unknown man, Martin said. He said the aircraft had been fitted with photographic equipment and shipped to Tucson, and that that was the last Martin knew of it.

There was little information on the exploits of the Mexican bomber until Masson and Dean returned a few months later with photos, scars, and souvenirs from their adventure. They reported some success, especially in Guaymas, where the bombs caused great panic among federal troops. And where the first deaths by aerial bombardment were recorded.

At one point, the enemy had had a chance to get rid of the aerial threat, but apparently was too fascinated by the contraption to set fire to it. Masson's engine had quit while he was on a flight over federal territory. He had glided to a landing, and he and Tommy Dean ran for the bush to hide. Dean pulled out the distributor cap and shoved it into his pocket—just in case one of the federal troops might know something about flying. Villa's cavalry swept through the region later, and the pilot and mechanic came back out of hiding. Masson and Dean survived the fighting, but they eventually had to steal horses and sneak back across the border in order to get away from the revolution.

Within a year, the world went to war, and the real battle of the clouds began.

3

Mitchell's
Martin Bomber

Twenty-two-year-old Lucille Mainwaring knew how to wear clothes and had a gaze that made men uneasy. Fresh out of secretarial school in 1914, she was on probation during her first weeks at the Glenn L. Martin Company. But there didn't seem to be any doubt that she had a permanent job.

Lucille liked the work and the excitement of having the company and its airplanes always on the front pages of the Los Angeles papers. But she found Martin an uncomfortable place to work. "Mr. Bell always surprises me. Why doesn't he stay in his office?" asked Lucille.

The other girl just shrugged. She had a crush on the company's energetic, constantly hustling twenty-year-old plant superintendent.

A few days later, Lucille once again was startled to look up to see Larry Bell standing at her side.

"What are you doing, Miss Mainwaring?"

"Frankly, Mr. Bell, I'm not accustomed to having people surprise me."

"Surprise?"

"Well, Mr. Bell, I mean, I'm just excitable."

"It won't happen any more, not if I have to wear a cowbell!"

Larry was blushing, and his boyish face was topped with curly black hair. Lucille laughed at the intensity of his expression.

Larry smiled and asked, "May I take you to lunch—just to patch things up?"

"I'd like that."

The next day, as Lucille and Larry walked down the street, she listened intently while he talked about the beginnings of a major war in Europe. "There's no doubt that airplanes are going to be able to control the flow of supplies and the movement of troops on the ground, someday."

Lucille nodded and engaged Larry's eyes with hers. He paused, and asked, "Dinner tonight?"

"Maybe we'd better have lunch first!"

They laughed and entered the neighborhood's favorite establishment for Texas hot dogs.

A few days later, Lucille looked up from her typing to see Larry standing in the door. In his hand was a silver charm bracelet bearing one lone ornament, a tiny cowbell.

"It's for you," said Bell.

Larry and Lucille were married on July 17, 1915. The next years were the happiest in their thirty-three-year marriage. Bell spent long hours in a woodworking shop he set up in the basement of their Los Angeles home. The couple raised pet dogs and often went out on Sundays in their new Ford.

They frequently went to baseball games. Bell followed big-league baseball closely and firmly believed that golf and baseball were the only worthwhile sports. Larry played in the annual Martin lunchtime softball league. Shirt sleeves rolled up, he took whatever position was available, although he liked pitching if somebody with superior talent wasn't around.

Bell was hot-tempered about the game, but he was a good sport. One day, Harry Ashburn of the Machine Shop tossed the ball hard at Larry and hit him in the face. The unexpected ball knocked Larry down. "I held my breath as Larry picked himself up out of the dust," Ashburn recalled, "but he just hollered, 'Let's play ball!' and nothing was said about it again."

Bell hadn't obtained his job as Martin's superintendent easily. A resignation had made the position available, and Bell went to Martin: "I can handle that job, Mr. Martin. You know I can."

"You're too young," replied the owner, who was thirty. "The job needs a man with seasoning." Larry had been crestfallen but agreed to continue as shop foreman. They discussed the kind of man that Martin had in mind and agreed the company could use someone with a formal engineering education. As acting superintendent, Bell was assigned to hire the man he would work for.

Larry, Glenn Martin, an unidentified man, and Donald Douglas with a propeller from the MB-2 bomber.

The army's Martin bombers sink the battleship Osfriesland.

The MB-2 over Washington, D.C.

Glenn Martin prepares for a filmmaking mission in one of his flights for a Hollywood studio.

The Martin office staff in 1917.

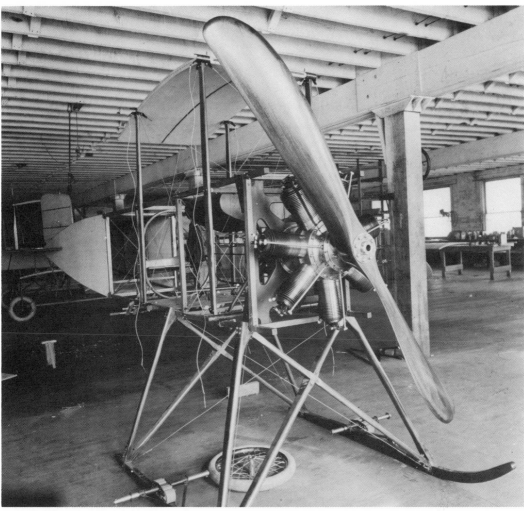

Single seat Martin biplane takes shape in the Los Angeles shop, about 1915. Cylinders and propeller spun around together in this model.

With the first twin-engine Martin bomber, from left, Larry Bell, test pilot Eric Springer, Glenn Martin, and Donald Douglas.

Instead of making the usual industry contacts, Larry wrote to the Massachusetts Institute of Technology, which had established a well-respected aviation engineering program. They recommended a graduate named Donald W. Douglas. "Mr. Douglas," Bell said at the first interview, "Mr. Martin has asked me to hire the man I'll be working for, and you're not going in to see him unless you prove you know more about airplanes than I do and prove you're better able to run this company than I am."

Larry was not a big man, only five-foot-six, but he had a capacity for engaging someone with bone-chilling directness. Young Douglas blinked. "Let's get at it," he said.

Bell grilled him on general knowledge of the state of the industry, then on detailed engineering concepts. Bell's mastery of the interview began to give way. There was nothing young Bell didn't know about airplane production, but he had some gaps on the engineering side of things. And he refused to bluff. Once, when Douglas talked at length in response to an engineering question, Larry couldn't resist pounding the table with the exclamation, "Dammit, you're right!"

The two men had talked for four hours when Larry suddenly said, "I think you're ready to see Mr. Martin."

It was sunset when Bell and Douglas walked into the owner's spotless office. Martin peered intently at Bell through polished eyeglasses. "Let me introduce Donald Douglas, who has qualifications that may interest you," Bell said. Upon previous agreement with Martin, Bell excused himself. It pained him, and he felt soreness in his throat at the realization that he had just moved one step lower in the organization. Alone, he walked out into the dark street, touching an eye with his wrist.

The next morning, Martin called Larry into his office. "You left too early last night, Bell," he said. "You weren't here for the announcement."

"What announcement?"

"You've been made superintendent of this company, and Donald Douglas has been named chief engineer."

Larry took to the job with demon energy. There seemed to be no detail that did not involve him in some way. He kept production running smoothly and had time to be chief salesman, contract writer, purchasing agent, and labor relations representative. In spare evenings, he worked long hours in his basement workshop, finishing oak dining room furniture he and Lucille had designed themselves.

Larry was friendly with employees but never discussed personal matters. Despite this, he seemed to know a tremendous amount about the lives of everyone around him. A young designer once met Larry in the hall the first day on the job, and the two introduced themselves. "Pleased to meet you; my name's Marcus O'Donnell," said the engineer. They chatted briefly about the bomber program, then parted.

A month later, the young engineer again met Bell in the hall. "Why, hello, O'Donnell, how've you been?" asked Larry. O'Donnell knew Bell was one of the executives but had completely forgotten his name. He murmured, "Working hard," and retreated to his drafting board.

When O'Donnell discussed the matter with a friend, he was told: "Larry Bell remembers everything."

In 1917, Martin made an error that ended his company. He decided to merge with the Wright Company. The idea was that the combination of Wright engines and Martin's aircraft know-how had the potential to be the most powerful aircraft company in the United States. It didn't work. Almost immediately after the merger, Wright-Martin received large orders for aircraft engines needed for the war effort overseas, and aircraft production was shoved aside. Martin and Bell became disgruntled and quit. Donald Douglas left for military service.

"We're still going to build airplanes," Martin told Bell, sending him to find a plant site and build a new factory in Cleveland, Ohio, where Martin had powerful financial backers. "While you're getting started, I'm going hunting for a contract."

Douglas returned to the company and, by the end of the war, had designed the United States' first twin-engine bomber, the Martin MB-2. It wasn't rolled out until after the war, but it proved versatile enough to serve a variety of postwar purposes, and the Glenn L. Martin Company went into production with the big open-cockpit airplane.

A draftsman named J. H. (Dutch) Kindelberger joined the company fresh out of army service. Two weeks later, he was still coming to work in his army uniform, and Larry kidded him: "What'm I supposed to do, salute?" "Plenty of wear left in these," said Kindelberger, who was not a man to waste money on frivolities.

Donald Douglas soon left because of a fight with Larry. They had gotten into a dispute over an engineering matter and had gone to Martin.

"If this is going to be done Bell's way," said Douglas, "I'm leaving." Douglas was the best designer Martin had had, but the owner showed no emotion: "If you feel that way about it, I guess there's nothing else for you to do."

In 1920, Douglas organized his own aircraft company in Santa Monica. Kindelberger joined him several years later, became vice president of engineering, and, in 1933, left Douglas to become elected president of the newly formed North American Aviation, Inc.

Larry became vice president and general manager of Martin's company, as well as chief contact man with the army during the final stages of developing the twin-engine bomber. It meant many trips to Wright Field at Dayton to see the head of the army's airplane section, Colonel Thurman H. Bane.

A day's business in Dayton required an all-night ride on the train from Cleveland. Arrival time was 5:00 A.M., so Larry had to sit in the lobby of the city's only hotel until the dining room opened at 7:30. After breakfast he rode a trolley to the airfield.

A major break came when the U.S. Postal Department bought six aircraft to expand on its fledgling airmail service, which had started with war-surplus Curtiss Jennies.

General Billy Mitchell was fascinated with the potential of the new bomber and often visited the plant to check on its progress. Once, at Larry's request, Mitchell gave his air-power talk before the Martin work force, standing in front of a bomber trimmed in stars and stripes.

Mitchell constantly spoke of the importance of aviation to the United States. In the 1920s, he predicted that United States indifference to airpower would some day encourage an attack by Japan on Hawaii that would cripple the U.S. fleet.

His ideas were seriously studied by military leaders in almost every nation but his own. And he was headed for deep trouble with his traditional-thinking superiors on Sunday, July 24, 1921, when he led six Martin bombers in the first demonstration of the capability of airplanes to sink battleships.

The U.S. military had turned down his idea of using the war-spoils German battleship *Osfriesland* for aerial attack trials. By international agreement at the end of World War I, the ship had to be scuttled, and the navy planned to do it with a bombardment by battleship guns. Mitchell went to Congress to get permission for the aerial experiment.

Billy Mitchell had closely followed the development of the

first 2,000 pound bomb and the only airplane capable of carrying it, the Martin bomber. He knew it could do the job. Admirals who witnessed the *Osfriesland* sinking shuddered the first time they saw one of the big bombs raise a mountain of water alongside the German battleship. Four more bombs were dropped at two minute intervals. Then the ship began to sink, slowly tipping to nearly perpendicular and then sliding under the surface.

The demonstration had a devastating effect. By exploding one ton bombs eighty feet underwater, the ship's vulnerable hull had been torn open in several places. These gaping holes were exposed as the ship upended for its final plunge beneath the surface. Until that moment, nothing short of a hurricane or a barrage by huge gun batteries had ever sunk a battleship. Six cloth-and-wood airplanes had done it in a few minutes' time.

Martin, who had witnessed the demonstration, called Bell at home from Washington that night with full details.

"Bell," said Martin, "now tell me what has been achieved in Cleveland in my absence."

Larry finished the report, hung up noisily, and then walked back into the living room. "He's getting on my nerves," he told Lucille. "I'm sick of this."

"Everyone who knows him respects him," said Lucille. "Why can't you get along?"

"Because everyone who knows what's going on thinks I ought to be company president," said Larry, snapping his newspaper.

There was a moment of silence. Larry glanced up in search of an expression of agreement on Lucille's face. There wasn't any. She admired Glenn Martin and respected him.

Larry boosted his career by accepting countless speaking engagements. In a leaflet promoting one of his talks, the Cleveland Industrial Alliance said: "Mr. Bell as a speaker has the rare gift of presenting cold facts in a most fascinating garb, and in relieving technical information with the brightest humor which will make this evening's contribution exceedingly 'easy to take.'"

The talks were to the point, and Larry's humor was based on his personal experience, not just jokes he'd heard. Bell had the gift of reaching everyone in the room personally. Men and women who heard Bell once would say years later, "I know Larry Bell."

Bell frequently expressed nostalgia for his youth in Mentone.

General Billy Mitchell speaks before the Martin workforce in Cleveland. Larry Bell, in business suit with his arms crossed, can be seen just behind the general.

Larry Bell in a brand new overcoat, 1920.

Martin's new plant in Cleveland, 1917.

Army pilot greeted by a local beauty during an "Around America Flight" about 1918 using a Martin Model GMB.

A conference in Larry Bell's office, October 1916.

Larry at his desk, 1917.

On the way home from a speaking engagement, he told Lucille, "Do you know, I still keep in touch with my friends there? My good friend Morrison Rockhill is becoming a very successful lawyer."

"I know, Larry."

"Growing up in a small town has many virtues," he said. "It's a great source of knowledge."

"I'm a city girl," she replied, "but I think I know what you mean. Denver has the same warmth as a small town."

"Youngsters in a small town," said Larry, "see a lot of things that in the city they wouldn't see. Everything is sort of camouflaged in the city, spread out and specialized, on the other block, or in some neighborhood where you never go.

"But that's not so in a small town. You see it all, as it actually is, not as somebody tries to pose it. You see what happens in the spring and in the fall, and you learn a lot about the things that have to be done in the spring and how you tend for the crops in the summer, harvest them in the fall, and then repair and prepare all winter.

"When you die in the city, they haul you away to a plot of dirt you've never seen. In the country, the earth's not so impersonal to you. It's a friend and provider through life and a resting place at death."

Larry and Lucille tried to have children but never succeeded. News of their friends' growing families was accepted warmly, but it produced a trace of strain on the faces of Mr. and Mrs. Bell.

Bell grew increasingly restless about his career. "I may quit Martin," he told Lucille one night. "If Grover were alive I'd be in business with him. The way it is, I'm number-two man, and I always will be."

Tension between Bell and Martin mounted. Larry felt he was important enough to the organization to become a part owner, at least in a small way, but Martin refused. In late 1924, Bell made an ultimatum. Either he was going to have a share in the ownership, or he would have to leave the company. "Then it looks like you'll have to leave," replied Martin. Bell departed on January 18, 1925.

On the last day in his office to pick up his personal items, Larry paused for a moment. As he looked around the room, it seemed shabby, the way last year's suit looks in the store mirror. "I can do better than this," said Bell, as he stood up abruptly and walked out the door.

The Bells returned to Los Angeles and lived at 3950 West 8th Street while Larry job-hunted for more than three years. The aircraft business wasn't hiring, so Larry sold machine tools for a while, then got into an unsuccessful scheme to look for a "lost gold mine" in a place called Mohawk, Arizona. Three men owned a map to the "mine," and Larry and two others contracted to use the map to find it. The split was to be six ways. When this effort folded, Larry got into an agreement with a man who had invented a "pencil-type" cigar lighter. The patent was assigned to Bell with the stipulation that he would develop it and sell it. This, too, was a failure, although Larry didn't let go of the idea for several years.

In early 1928, the aircraft industry slump had ended, and Larry developed three job possibilities. He was offered a position as factory manager for Boeing in Seattle, sales manager for Consolidated Aircraft in Buffalo, or president of a small airplane company in Buffalo. The last option had him interested, but the small company folded while Bell was still pondering its possibilities. Lucille breathed a sigh of relief. Buffalo was the last place she wanted to go.

But in Buffalo, Major Reuben H. Fleet (U.S. Army, Retired), president of Consolidated, had decided he needed Bell for his ability as a manager-salesman. Fleet and Bell settled the agreement by phone. Larry was to start on July 1, 1928, at $7,500 a year. He also could purchase 2 percent of Consolidated's stock for $25,000, payable at $100 a month from his salary, along with any dividends declared. Annual interest was 6 percent on the unpaid balance. The same offer applied to a smaller Fleet enterprise, Tonawanda Products Corp.

The key phrase in the agreement for Larry was this: "You [will have] a substantial interest in the company with and for which you will be working." Bell was about to become a capitalist.

Now came the task of telling Lucille, who was reading a copy of *Colliers* when Larry walked through the door. "How would you like to move to Buffalo?" Lucille threw down the magazine and left the room. Larry had one final sales job on his hands before the Bells started their new life on Lake Erie's shore.

4

An Idea
Comes of Age

"I'll bet you a thousand dollars to a buck that you can't get one flying by Christmas," Major Fleet told Larry as they walked across the busy production floor. Larry had been sizing up the assembly line and had a good gut feeling about what he saw. Fleet was building the first PY-1 amphibious aircraft, named "flying boats," and they were beautifully designed machines. "What do you say, Bell?" the major asked impatiently.

"It's a bet," said Larry.

Bell was impressed—almost overwhelmed—by Major Fleet in those first days of working for the man. The lean, aggressive company president never stopped talking. He had endless ideas. Larry himself was a prodigious talker and storyteller, but the major left him speechless.

Fleet was involved in a big gamble. He was organizing a new airline, NYRBA (New York-Rio-Buenos Aires), to fly his new PY-1s. He needed help in running his plant while he was busy elsewhere.

Larry had a lot to learn about the plant built on the site of the original World War I Curtiss "Jenny" factory at 2050 Elmwood Avenue, but Bell felt at home. Fleet's airplanes were being built with craftsmanship. The company's major product, the PT "Husky" primary trainer, was becoming the United States' top military trainer.

The new product, however, was flying boats, and Larry made sure the takeoff of PY-1 No. 1 from Lake Erie took place in the first week of December. Bell collected his bet and was promoted to vice president. Larry had teamed with the assistant general manager, Ray P. Whitman, to keep things running smoothly. Bell, Whitman, and Fleet held an after-dinner meeting in the plant in early 1929 to discuss progress of another new airplane to be introduced that year, the "Fleetster."

"This'll be the first time anyone's gone into production with an all-metal airplane," said Major Fleet. "Do you see any problems?"

"No," said Larry. "Ray and I are of the opinion that it's going to simplify the production process."

"It's a direct takeoff from the flying boats," said Whitman.

Fleet leaned back in his huge swivel chair. "I'm relying on you two. Frankly, I'm spread thinner than ever. These new products take a lot of attention. So does the NYRBA. I'm going to be out of town a lot."

"We'll keep things moving," said Bell.

Major Reuben Fleet had gained fame in the U.S. Army after World War I as a flyer and can-do officer. He had organized the first U.S. air mail service in only nine days in 1918. This kind of background made Fleet the ideal executive in the eyes of Bell and Whitman. Bell had become especially sensitive to the fact that the industry leaders he most admired had flying backgrounds. And once on the shop floor he overheard his name mentioned in a way that made him uneasy: "Bell doesn't fly planes. He just builds 'em."

Bell joined the Aero Club of Buffalo the same day.

"These warm days are perfect for a long-distance ride," a balloonist named George Hineman told Bell one afternoon. "Let's spend the weekend aloft. You'll travel farther than you would in a year in railroad trains."

Hineman was a veteran of lighter-than-air craft and owned a huge red, white, and blue balloon that he kept at the airport. With two friends, Larry scheduled a flight early one Saturday in May, 1929. Lucille drove Larry to the airport and stayed behind to watch the liftoff.

"Larry, why are you doing this?" she asked. "I think you're losing your mind."

"Safer than cars," Bell said, grinning as he strapped on a leather helmet.

The balloon lifted smoothly from the earth. Bell didn't realize, at first, that the balloon was airborne—he was looking up inside the balloon, studying the way it was made. Hineman nudged him: "Hey, Larry! Look down."

Bell's hands tightened their grip. He was one hundred feet above the earth.

The breeze aloft was strong from the southeast. In minutes, the small party was over Lake Ontario and headed for Canada. At an altitude of three thousand feet near Galt, Ontario, the balloon sagged. "She's valving out!" shouted Hineman as he alternately tugged and released the control cord in an attempt to close the stuck valve.

The balloon descended to about one hundred feet and skimmed swiftly over a field toward some trees. The basket slammed into the upper branches of a massive elm and snagged while the balloon limply fluttered above.

"Not enough gas left to pull us free," said Hineman. "Hold on!" he shouted, pulling the valve cord. The balloon rapidly lost all its lift and the weight of the basket made it tumble through the tree safely to the ground.

The story of the balloon ride gave Bell a reputation as a flyer among the workers at Consolidated. From that time on, Bell made a point of flying in nearly every aircraft he produced, even when it meant installing a special seat.

"How would you like to be a company president?" Fleet asked Larry when the two met after a lengthy session of the board of directors.

"I think I'd like that," said Bell.

Fleet outlined his plan. He personally would buy the rights to the "Husky Junior," rename it the "Fleet" and manufacture it at a new subsidiary company to be known as Fleet Aircraft. "You can be president of Fleet Aircraft if you want the job," said the major.

Fleet Aircraft bought land in Fort Erie, Ontario, just across the Peace Bridge from Buffalo, and built a plant and airstrip there. The small two-place biplane rapidly became a popular sports and training aircraft.

Reuben Fleet demonstrated the Fleet coast to coast in 1929 in a typically bold way. He took his secretary and personal friend, Lauretta Lederer Golem, on a Fleet trip from airport to airport around the country, including the National Air Races at Los Angeles.

On Friday, September 13, Fleet called Larry from Detroit. "We're on the last leg, Larry. Meet me at the airport, will you? We'll arrive at about four."

Bell was alone in his car at Consolidated's Military Road airstrip when his new young secretary, Irene Bernhardt, drove over from the plant and parked next to him: "Mr. Bell, there's been an accident. Major Fleet and his secretary are in a hospital in London, Ontario."

Larry quickly made arrangements to drive Lauretta's mother to the hospital. It was tense. Larry knew that Lauretta's neck was broken, and she might be dead by the time they arrived, but her mother knew only that Lauretta was injured.

In the meantime, the company sent two of Buffalo's best surgeons north in a pair of PT-3s. Both doctors were shaken and airsick when they arrived. They had encountered bad weather and had landed in a wheatfield enroute to ask directions from a farmer. Lauretta died that Saturday. Major Fleet had kidney injuries and a broken leg. "Get my family here," Fleet told Bell. Larry stayed in London until the Fleets arrived, then returned to Buffalo to attend the funeral of thirty-one-year-old Lauretta Golem.

After flying thousands of miles in all kinds of weather, the major and his secretary had been the victims of engine failure. The crash had occurred when Fleet, battling to make a forced landing in a field, turned the aircraft so it would be heading into the wind. There hadn't been enough power in the engine, and the aircraft had dived nearly straight into the ground. After an investigation, Consolidated test pilot William B. Wheatley reported at the coroner's inquest that one small part, a rocker valve, had failed in one of the cylinders.

When Major Fleet returned to work after seven weeks in the hospital, he called a meeting of Consolidated's top executives to announce his decision to promote Bell to general manager. "I'm relying on you," he told Larry. "My health isn't up to par, and I've got to have time to heal."

Larry did some maneuvering to win new business for the company. Robert J. Woods, a brilliant design engineer employed by the old Lockheed Aircraft Corporation (purchased later by the present Lockheed), had designed a sleek pursuit aircraft—the XP-900—from Lockheed's successful low-wing monoplane "Sirius."

A prototype successfully completed tests at Wright Field, and the army immediately issued a contract for five service test models, to be known as the YP-25.

Lockheed's parent company, Detroit Aircraft Corporation, fell into financial difficulty, suddenly leaving the army with no source of supply for its YP-25s. A scramble for the job took place in the aircraft industry, and Larry decided Consolidated needed it most. He got in touch with friends on the West Coast and learned that Bob Woods was headed for Detroit by train. Bell immediately boarded a train west.

When Woods's train arrived in Chicago a few days later, he was surprised to hear a pageboy calling out his name. The message was to meet a Mr. Bell at the information counter.

"How do you do, Mr. Woods," said Larry as Woods walked up. "My name's Larry Bell, and I've got a proposition for you."

The two men took a liking to each other, and Woods signed a contract to go to work for Consolidated. While Woods boarded the train for Buffalo, Larry headed toward Wright Field with the contract in his pocket. Consolidated won the YP-25 job and gained the services of one of the industry's most creative design engineers.

On the commercial side, Consolidated's "Fleetster" was becoming a solid success. This airplane could carry eight or nine passengers and a load of mail at 160 mph. Several airlines were buying "Fleetsters."

But flying boats had become the major product. The Navy was putting P2Y-1 "Rangers" through a series of long-distance formation flights that gained world attention. On January 10, 1934, Navy Patrol Squadron VP-10 flew six aircraft through a long night of thick overcast to make it to Pearl Harbor from San Francisco in twenty-five hours. The 2,408 mile flight was termed a "magnificent accomplishment" by President Roosevelt. Crowds cheered as the navy planes taxied up out of the water.

The most famous version of the Consolidated flying boat was still in the design stages. The PBY "Catalina," which was to play an important role in World War II, was the creation sign of I. M. (Mac) Laddon, America's foremost designer of flying boats. Mac Laddon had also designed the "Fleetster."

Consolidated had become one of the nation's most successful military aircraft manufacturers, but both Bell and Reuben Fleet were restless. Fleet wanted to move to a climate where his airplanes could operate from water twelve months a year—not sit on ramps through Buffalo's long winter, waiting for Lake Erie to thaw.

And Bell yearned to build a company of his own. "I've developed a yen to prove whether I'm going to be a number one man, or whether I'm going to be a number two man all my life," he told Lucille.

Larry made a trip to Detroit and Chicago to meet potential

backers who might help him go into business in one of those cities. When he asked about start-up capital, the reply was always the same. "You're well known in Buffalo. That's your base. That's where you'll find capital." "My hands are tied," he told Lucille. "I can't open up across the street from Consolidated. Major Fleet is a good friend. No one would want to buy my stock and take sides between the major and me. What I have to do is convince the major to move out of town. He's already looking, anyway."

Some years earlier, Major Fleet had taken an option on a small site at Long Beach, California, a mile or so from the ocean. In 1934, he and his new wife, Dorothy Mitchell Fleet, traveled to California with Larry and Lucille to take a look at the location; but, after one day in Long Beach, it was agreed that the site wouldn't do. Something closer to the ocean was needed.

The two businessmen found what they wanted in San Diego. Bell had recommended this city, knowing that Fleet was nostalgic for the place where he had learned to fly during his early army days. After initial meetings with city leaders, the Fleets departed for Buffalo, leaving Larry and Lucille in San Diego to complete the arrangements, which included use of a large tract of land on Pacific Boulevard adjacent to Lindbergh Field, as well as several acres on the other side of the street.

The land wasn't available for outright purchase, but Consolidated could have it on a ninety-nine-year lease. Bell and San Diego's officials prepared a lease for $1,000 a year. San Diego's officials were anxious to bring prime industry to town, and an aircraft plant would be ideal.

When Bell showed Major Fleet the lease, Fleet shook his head in disbelief. "You've driven too hard a bargain," he said, crossing out the $1,000 and changing it to $10,000. "That's more like a fair deal."

Consolidated quietly made preparations to move out of Buffalo on July 1, 1935. Ray Whitman and Larry Bell just as quietly made plans to form a company to replace Consolidated in Buffalo. "Larry and I had the same idea at the same time," Whitman recalled in 1976. "We discussed the possibility every chance we had. Almost every time we were in town together, we had lunch at the Park Lane Restaurant, where we could talk undisturbed. Many a luncheon tablecloth bore our sketches and writing."

In the midst of all the planning, there was a tug-of-war between Larry and Ray over what to name the new company. "I wanted something more general than Bell Aircraft," said Whitman. Bell held that almost every major airplane company bore a founder's name. "It's a personal thing with the people who started the airplane business, beginning with the Wrights," said Bell. "The experience connected with my name will help give us a strong start."

There had been some mention of the name Frontier Aircraft, but Larry said he had been told by one businessman to "put your name on it, and I'll invest."

As soon as Consolidated announced its intention to move, Bell openly contacted friends and businessmen about the possibility of backing a new aircraft plant. Design engineer Woods joined the venture, and Bell's secretary, Irene Bernhardt, also stayed on as secretary for the new company.

For Buffalo, the news that Consolidated was leaving town had been a shock. In the midst of growing unemployment and business failure, Consolidated had been one of the few expanding, successful local companies. Of slightly more than one thousand employees, 411 would move to California, leaving the rest unemployed in Buffalo.

Bell's plan was welcome. He met with city officials and the publishers of the major dailies, the *Buffalo Evening News*, the *Courier-Express* and the *Times*. Everywhere the reply was the same: "Let us know what we can do to help."

Earlier in the year, Larry and Major Fleet had met privately in the Buffalo Club. Bell outlined his tentative plans at that session and had won the support of the major.

"There'll be a strong nucleus for a new company left behind, and there are signs that the city's leading people will give all-out support," Bell said.

"Frankly, I've felt you bucking for your own company for two years now," said Fleet. "I know the feeling. Keep in mind that Consolidated will be busy moving men and equipment three thousand miles during the next few months. We've got a lot of work to do just accomplishing that. Some subcontracting may be available for a smart young company."

"I've considered that possibility."

"I bet you have, Bell."

Major Fleet was deeply disappointed at the news that Whitman also planned to stay in Buffalo. Whitman had been with

Larry and Lucille ready to board the "Fleetster."

The plant where Bob Woods startled the world with his advanced airplane designs in the 1930s, 2050 Elmwood Ave., Buffalo. Only the mail truck was behind the times.

The Gwynn Aircar developed by Larry's former chief engineer from Consolidated, Joseph M. Gwynn, who formed the Gwynn Aircar Co. in 1935.

One of the Consolidated P-30s built in Buffalo before the work was transferred to California in 1935.

Larry, at left, is in his element with the Bell people at a summer picnic in the 1930s. Wearing the camera is his assistant, Dave Forman.

With the "Fleetster," Consolidated test pilot Bill Wheatley is at far right and pilot Bert Acosta is next to him with Larry Bell at center. The others are unidentified.

Fleet since 1925 and was an important part of the major's plans for the future. "Make the move with us," said Fleet, "and you've got a job as manager."

"My mind is made up," said Whitman.

An emotional man, there were tears in Major Fleet's eyes as the two men shook hands in farewell. "I'll always have an opening if you ever regret your decision," said Major Fleet.

On June 20, 1935, Larry submitted his formal resignation, along with Bob Woods and Irene Bernhardt. By arrangement, Ray Whitman remained a Consolidated employee to supervise the shutdown of Consolidated's Buffalo operation.

"At least one of us has a paying job," Whitman kidded Bell on the morning of Friday, June 21.

"I feel like I'm on gas," said Bell, "Like that balloon ride, we're on our own."

On Sunday, June 30, the *Courier-Express* ran the story by reporter Ann McIlhenney: "Buffalo will be kept on the map as a hub of the aviation manufacturing industry." The article included a paragraph stating that the new aircraft company "has obtained complete financial backing from leading wealthy citizens of Buffalo."

In San Diego, Major Fleet opened his new factory at ceremonies before a crowd of thirty thousand. His dedication speech praised San Diego for "all-year-round flying weather for test flying and flight deliveries, in a city large enough to furnish a reasonable supply of labor and materials, with a climate unhampered by snow and ice."

In Buffalo, a chill descended on the new company. They received word that Major Fleet had decided to take a contract for fifty P-30 pursuit planes with him, despite his indication that this work would be left behind. Without that contract, the new aircraft company was going to have to be sold to investors on the basis of the founders' reputations alone.

5

Bell Aircraft
Is Born

Washington Street was burning in midsummer sunshine when Larry stepped out of the carved-wood coolness of the Lafayette Hotel restaurant. The sudden brilliance stunned him, and his step faltered as he headed for a telephone booth on the corner. He had a cramp in his stomach, and he breathed in gasps as he dialed Bell Aircraft Corporation's tiny offices at 1807 Elmwood Ave.

"Irene, have there been any calls?"

"No, Mr. Bell. Not once since you left at eleven."

"Will you put Ray on? . . . Ray, I got nowhere with those guys. All kinds of enthusiasm but not a dollar hard cash."

"We were counting on them, Larry."

The dingy phone booth was in full sunlight, and Larry was sweating. His voice lowered to a whisper. "Ray, it's been nineteen days. We haven't sold anything for nineteen days in a row. We're in trouble. Wait at the office until I get back."

Larry pushed open the phone booth door and held it open with his foot to let in some fresh air while he dialed Lucille at home. "Any calls, Lucille?"

"Just one from your friend, John Garver. He says he's talked to someone who may be interested in buying stock."

"Did he mention a name?"

"Yes, it's Shelton Weed, owner of that big hardware store on Main Street."

"I'll call Garver right away. But first I'm going to get something for my stomach. It hurt like hell at lunch today."

53

"Oh, Larry, I wish you'd see a doctor."

"I'll need more than a doctor if things don't pick up, Lucille," he said as he hung up and headed toward a drug store up the street.

At first, it had seemed easy. In June, the founders had rented two small offices at only $35 a month, installed a telephone, and helped Bob Woods set up his design boards. Then, on July 10, 1935, Bell Aircraft Corporation was legally founded when Ansley W. Sawyer filed papers in Albany.

The new company was capitalized at $500,000; a start-up minimum of $150,000 had to be raised by September 1. If the deadline was not met, the company would instantly become one more in the long string of business ventures to die in the years of the Great Depression.

But the Bell venture seemed to have made a solid start. At the end of the first week, Larry, Ray, Woods, Irene, and a former assistant treasurer at Consolidated, Charles L. Beard, counted $90,000 in cash and subscriptions. It was mostly their own money. The first outsider to buy shares was an insurance man named Henry Holland, who subscribed for $10,000—the price for 100 shares of Bell Aircraft preferred stock at $100 a share, plus 100 shares of common stock as a bonus.

But suddenly, the well ran dry. Day after day went by without a sale. "It boils down to this," Bell said at a morning meeting. "The prominent Buffalo citizens who urged us to start this are now crying broke."

"Can it be possible?" asked Whitman.

"I've gotten ahold of some bankers to help tell us the sheep from the goats," said Larry.

He tried various techniques to win investor confidence. Larry did push ups in one office, when his health was questioned. Elsewhere, he offered a life insurance policy made out to the investor. "Even if I die, you don't lose," he said.

Lucille worried about just that. Larry was losing weight, chain-smoking, and never seemed to sleep. Late one night, she walked into the kitchen of their apartment at 33 Gates Circle and stood silently watching him taking notes from various scraps of paper. The room was blue with smoke, and a half-empty glass of scotch rested precariously on the edge of the kitchen table.

Without speaking, Lucille cleaned up around her husband, emptied the ash tray and replaced the drink with a glass of milk.

She stood next to him. As Larry wearily looked up, she said, "Come to bed. You'll be able to think better in the morning."

"Not now. I'll be done in a few minutes. I'm onto something here."

The gloom deepened as day after day in August went by. One morning, just as he was about to leave, Lucille asked Larry how things were going. "My dear wife," said Bell, "we are now ringing doorbells one by one."

On August 15, 1935, the world was shocked to hear that Wiley Post and Will Rogers had been killed in an airplane crash. "That's a tragedy for us all," said Bell. But it was later that same day Larry had his appointment to see the wealthy Shelton Weed.

Larry was in top form, outlining the possibilities of his company. As he listened, Weed silently moved his checkbook to the center of his desk and began writing. Larry paused. When Weed handed him the check, Larry was stunned: $10,000, and the man hadn't asked a single question. Bell looked puzzled.

"Don't you remember me, Larry?"

"I honestly don't, Mr. Weed."

"Well, I remember you. When you were president of the Aero Club some years back, you wrote to me for a $100 loan to help fund an air show. I sent you the money and forgot about it. I often make contributions to civic ventures and never see the cash again. Yours was the only money that ever came back."

"I remember now. That air show paid its own way."

"I've been in business for fifty years," said Weed. "I've underwritten everything you can think of, and I've heard all kinds of promises. Yours was kept. I'll trust you again."

Weed put his reputation behind Bell, promoting the new company among his business acquaintances and in places like the Buffalo Club and Saturn Club. Money began to come in. Charles A. Criqui, president of Sterling Engine Company, bought 200 shares, then Weed signed up for another 150.

The $150,000 start-up mark was passed, and Bell Aircraft was in business. Later, Bell recalled that he had never worried or worked harder than he did in the weeks between July 10 and mid-August 1935, "and an ulcer was born."

The company was set up with Bell as president and Whitman as vice president, treasurer, and purchasing agent. Woods was chief design engineer. Beard was named secretary and assistant treasurer.

Part of the former Consolidated plant was rented for a year from the American Radiator Company for 100 shares of stock.

Furniture was needed, so the staff went shopping. There were two rules: no desk was to cost more than $5 and no chair more than $2. Bell later enjoyed asking guests how much he thought he'd paid for his battered desk. They always quoted high. "Five bucks. That's all. Isn't it a beauty?" asked Bell.

Several employees were hired, and the plant went to work making exhaust pipes and radio masts under subcontract to local firms.

Bell Aircraft held design and manufacturing rights for a biplane, the Great Lakes BG-1 dive bomber. Little was done with this license, but it helped morale to have an aircraft on the premises.

Bell was frequently out in the shop talking to the production men. "Buffalo Germans," he said, walking past Irene's desk. "No craftsmen in the world better than those guys."

Consolidated had nine million dollars in backlog orders when it left Buffalo. It was building PB-2As, the airplanes designed by Bob Woods for the army, and navy PBY-1 flying boats under the largest U.S. government contract for aircraft since World War I. Consolidated was still unsettled in San Diego, however, and needed help. In January 1936, Bell Aircraft got a small contract, then an order came in for 144 wing panels for PBY-2s and 3s, total: $890,000.

The first modern airplane to arrive at the Buffalo plant was an attack version of the Consolidated PB-2Y, designated the A-11A. The air corps was impressed with the potential of the Allison V-1710 12-cylinder, 1,000-horsepower engine and had announced it was willing to spend $25,000 to have one installed experimentally in the A-11A. Bell Aircraft used Bob Woods's experience as an ace card in winning the job.

Larry cut red tape by knocking $5 off the Bell bid, since contracts of $25,000 or more required clearance through a number of channels in Washington. The engine and aircraft were at the Bell plant in a matter of weeks.

The odd work and subcontracts provided funds to meet the payroll, but the Allison engine project was to be a key to Bell's future. The experience gained on the A-11A was useful in the design of the first Bell-built aircraft, the YFM-1 Airacuda.

A board of directors for the new company was selected on October 15 at the first shareholders' meeting in the Elmwood plant. The group gathered quietly and sat on fold-open chairs. "As you know," said Bell, "three members of the board will come from management. That is myself, Ray Whitman, and Bob Woods. The other four members will be shareholders selected by you today."

The three management representatives left the room while the matter was discussed. When they were called back, Ansley Sawyer told them, "We've decided to accept management's recommendations. Name your own board."

The shareholders took a plant tour, while Bell, Whitman, and Woods discussed their choices for directorship. Outside, the small group walked through the old factory building, solemnly looking at the collection of battered furniture and well-worn machinery. "They don't build stuff this tough anymore," said one investor, hopefully. When the board reconvened, one vote elected the following slate: Bell, Whitman, Woods, Ansley Sawyer, Walter A. Yates, Charles Criqui, and W. A. Van Arsdale.

The company's first annual report, dated March 25, 1936, listed a net loss of $5,843.02 for the period July 10 to December 31, 1935. It noted that, at the end of the year, there were forty-eight shareholders owning 3,098 preferred and common shares.

In his letter, Larry had encouraging words:

"A contract for the modification of an army A-11 airplane, in the amount of $24,995, is scheduled to be completed next month. On March 4, 1936, the corporation delivered engineering work to the army air corps in the amount of $39,000.

"On January 28, 1935 [sic] the corporation contracted with Consolidated Aircraft Corporation of San Diego, California, to manufacture 146 outboard wing panels and parts therefore for U.S. Navy Patrol flying boats. The contract is in the total amount of $878,330.38 less 5 percent; deliveries to start in June 1936 and to be completed in April 1937.

"The Corporation has 167 employees as of today; more are being employed to handle work on hand. The necessary additional equipment is being installed. The corporation's initial plant of 40,000 ft., under lease for two years from January 1, 1936, has been increased by an additional 40,000 ft., under lease for one year beginning April 1, 1936."

Additions to the Bell work force were not made haphazardly. Young, creative engineers were drawn to the company by Bob

Woods's reputation. And Larry's personal salesmanship attracted executive candidates. J. Frederick Schoellkopf IV, whose forebears developed the giant Niagara Falls hydro-electric works, was one of Larry's proteges. So was another offspring of a prominent Buffalo family, David G. Forman. The two young men could have had jobs in all types of established companies but started with Bell Aircraft at low pay because of the future they saw with Larry Bell. (Forman recalled in 1976 that he had started with Bell at $26 a week.)

6

A Tiger
with Teeth

Larry walked into Bob Woods's office brandishing a pad of
yellow legal paper in front of him like a rapier. "I've got it all
here," he said excitedly, as Woods looked up in surprise.
"Here's what the Army wants, and nobody else is anywhere
close to giving it to them."

Shoving aside papers and putting his notepad in the center of
the desk, Bell pointed at a list he had written:

—Top priority, get a cannon in the sky, knockout punch.
—High speed, use *two* Allison pushers.
—Escort, attack, bomber rolled into one.

"We've been putting pop guns on airplanes. Thirty calibers.
That's like throwing rice," said Bell. "It's time to design a
flying platform and put cannons on it."

Woods pulled a drawing out from under his blotter. "Does
this look like the ship?"

Bell checked it over intently, smoothing wrinkles with his
hands as he studied each detail. Moving a forefinger from point
to point, he murmured, "Huh," and asked, "What's this?" or
"What powers that?" Finally: "Bob, it's clean. And that punch
ought to do the job." "Where did you ever get an idea like
this?"

"It was your idea," said Woods. "Remember—find the right
armament and build around it?"

"I remember, but I didn't foresee anything like this!"

Bell walked out with the drawing, leaving his note pad

behind. Woods rearranged his desk and put Larry's notepad in the "out" basket; Irene would know where it came from.

Back in his office, Bell had the drawing spread out on his desk. "Airacuda," said Larry to himself. "Like the barracuda: sleek, shiny, and big sharp teeth!"

Woods's design had been made in response to a trend of thought in the army. Early in 1935, a young flyer, Captain Harry A. Johnson, had written to chief of the air corps Major General Benjamin Foulis recommending development of a heavily-armed super fighter capable of destroying bombers. Hap Arnold had expressed dissatisfaction with existing pursuit aircraft for some time, but Captain Johnson's letter is believed to be the document that set the wheels in motion.

The airplane was to have a new designation: FM—for "fighter, multi-place." When informed that Bell Aircraft had come up with a design, the military had good reason to take interest.

Woods was one of the designers the army watched closely. Between 1932 and 1935 at Consolidated, he had designed, in addition to the YIP-25, fastest military airplane in the world, the P-30, the PB-2A, and the A-11, fastest attack plane. Previously, as project engineer at Lockheed, he had designed the P-24 pursuit and the A-9 attack planes, and had done preliminary designs on the Vultee VT-1 transport, one of the most successful single-engine transports ever built.

Bell and Lockheed Aircraft submitted studies, and both companies were put under $25,000 contracts to perform preliminary engineering. Deadline was March 15, 1936.

Bell won the competition by four-tenths of a point, 72 to 71.6, out of a possible 100 points. The clincher apparently was the big twin guns aboard the Airacuda. Lockheed's aircraft had two 1,000-horsepower Allison engines, as did the Airacuda, but it had only one cannon. Lockheed held the edge in engineering, but Bell scored 19.3 to 15.6 in military characteristics.

The victory put Bell into phase two—building a mock-up and performing static tests; but the army held the option to shut down the program at any time. That put Ray Whitman, Bob Woods, and YFM-1 project engineer Art Fornoff under constant pressure at the plant, while Bell kept the sales effort going within the army.

On one visit to Wright Field, Bell had laid out his plans before a chief engineer.

"Very progressive," said the colonel. "It's got fire control, range-finding devices, auxiliary engines to run the electrical equipment. Unfortunately, we can't buy it. There's no military requirement."

"Military requirement?" asked Bell.

"It's like a requisition for material."

"Okay," said Larry, "can you tell me where I can get it?"

"From General Andrews at Langley Field."

Getting through to General Andrews was not easy. Bell spent several days showing his plans to various officers who worked for the general; but, finally, Andrews and his staff met with Bell to hammer out their questions and doubts.

Brigadier General Frank M. Andrews had been on record in favor of development of flying artillery for several months, but it took some convincing before he was to agree that the Airacuda was the answer.

Larry was at his best. He spoke at length about the big guns and how their range would allow the Airacuda to stand off two miles—far out of range of the smaller caliber defensive weapons of the bombers—and break up bomber squadrons. The FM could harass them with superior speed, downing them with tremendous gunpower fired remotely from the cockpit.

"But what about some rearward armament," asked a young colonel. "We ought to have some guns to protect the rear as well as having all that punch up front."

"What do you think, Larry?" General Andrews asked, as perspiration began to show on Bell's forehead.

"We have no provision for guns in the back," Bell said firmly, "because this airplane is fast enough to keep out of trouble. Nobody catches the fastest kid on the block."

The staff wasn't satisfied. They were pilots, and they were intent on protecting the men who would fly the FM—and that meant armament in all directions: no blind spots—especially in the rear.

Bell was outnumbered and running out of talk. His airplane was overweight already, and guns in the rear would cut performance even further. There was an uneasy silence; then suddenly he blurted:

"Look, guns in the rear makes about as much sense as putting teeth in the ass of a tiger. You put the teeth in the mouth!"

The remark brought a laugh and broke the tension for the moment, and Bell was off the spot. Intense questions continued for several days, and the prospects for the Airacuda seemed dim. General Andrews had not made himself available to Bell, until one day after a morning session: "Larry, let's go play golf."

After a day at the Yorktown Golf Course, the general held a formal dinner for Larry and the staff of officers. Throughout the meal, Bell sensed something was in the air.

"I'd like to make a toast," said the general after dinner. The room became silent. He looked over at Larry and continued: "I just want to drink a toast. I do that because we just decided today, my staff and I, to buy the Airacuda."

Bell hurried back to Buffalo to let his staff know the details, then went to Wright Field to be there when the military requirement documents arrived from Langley.

"They're on their way," said the colonel. "But you're only half-way home, Larry."

"Half-way what?"

"We can't buy anything without a military directive."

"A directive?" asked Bell. "Okay. I'm getting used to this. Now tell me two things. Where do I get a directive, and are there any more things I've got to get before we go to work?"

The colonel assured Bell that the directive would allow Wright Field to negotiate a contract. Getting it meant one more trip to Washington. A week later, in Ray Whitman's office, Bell said, "We're getting there at last. We've got the military requirement, and today the directive came in. Now all we've got to do is get the order. And then we're going to build a hell of an airplane."

Bell Aircraft had expanded almost from the beginning. By the end of 1935, the company had 56 employees and a backlog of $60,000. At the end of the next year it would have 642 employees and a $2.1 million backlog. The company leased additional buildings at the Elmwood Avenue location and, by the end of 1936, had 145,000 square feet of floor space. In 1936, Bell sent letters to the shareholders announcing a special meeting, July 20, at which they would be asked to act on a plan for recapitalizing to pay for this expansion.

"The management believes it possible to obtain additional business of a substantial character, requiring a considerable amount of new capital," said Bell in his letter, "and the board of directors is of the opinion that the company should be placed in a position to take advantage of the present demand for airplanes by obtaining new money without delay."

The plan involved an underwriting agreement with a group headed by G. M. P. Murphy & Company of New York City. The arrangement—worked out by Ansley Sawyer and his young associate, Mason O. Damon—would bring Bell Aircraft $500,000 in needed extra cash.

It was a touchy period for the new company. Bell needed the unanimous consent of seventy-five shareholders—the men and women who owned 3,660 preferred and common shares. The problem was this: the shareholders had to agree to abolish their preemptive rights to purchase their share of any increased stock. All seventy-five signed on the dotted line. They had trusted Bell from the start, and now he advised them: "As an example of the result of this transaction, a stockholder now owning 100 shares of preferred and 100 shares of common stock for which he paid $10,000 may either obtain 2,000 shares of the new stock or may offer to the company the new common stock issued in exchange for his preferred stock for $10,000 (his total investment) and obtain 1,000 shares of the new stock."

Over coffee and cigarettes in the Lafayette Hotel that summer, attorney Mason Damon put it in plain language for one of the shareholders:

"Last year you paid $100 for a share of preferred stock. That share would now become twenty shares of the new common stock, and the underwriters are offering the new stock at $12 a share. So your original $100 becomes worth something in the neighborhood of $240. You're not going to do too badly."

The company began construction of the first Airacuda in May 1936 under $25,000 allotted by the army for phase three of the FM program. The XFM-1's radical design incorporated several engineering innovations.

Bell engineers frequently visited the Colt firearms plant in Hartford, Connecticut, where Colt's off-the-shelf M1E1 37mm anti-aircraft gun was being redesigned to fit the Airacuda nacelles. These cannons could be fired by the gunner in the nacelle or by the navigator through a central fire control system that moved simultaneously through a 25-degree cone of fire. Electrically-powered gear trains controlled the gun turrets, but the guns themselves were in fixed mounts. (First gun delivery would not come until April 20, 1939.)

Woods had designed a pusher aircraft. Allison engines were installed in the rear of each nacelle and turned sixty-four-inch extension shafts to the propellers.

The Airacuda was a fountainhead of advanced aviation

concepts because its unconventional design required an endless amount of creative problem-solving.

The use of sixty-four-inch drive shafts, for example, was an innovation dreamed up to solve the problem of where to place the engines and still leave room for the cannons and the crewmen.

The Airacuda's tremendous firepower also required improved gun mounts. Available mounts were equipped with springs to absorb recoil and weren't rugged enough to handle 50-caliber guns. (Even with 30-caliber weapons, existing mounts tended to bounce and toss bullets all over the sky.)

A team headed by Bob Woods developed the first hydraulic, flexible gun mount. Automobile hydraulic shock absorbers were tested, and gradually Bell developed a gun mount that was smaller, lighter, and more accurate than the spring recoil type. The mount would become a Bell product and eventually resulted in an entire Bell division.

Working with Woods in developing the Bell gun mount were J. Fred Schoellkopf IV, Herbert S. Bowers, Art Fornoff, and F. M. Salisbury. It was Schoellkopf who apparently suggested the use of shock absorbers.

The Airacuda project was secret until the wings and fuselage were trucked out of the plant on July 19, 1937, and taken to a hangar at Buffalo Airport for final assembly. Newspapers kept track of progress with the airplane from that time on and on September 1, Lieutenant Benjamin S. Kelsey climbed into the cockpit for the first test flight.

The big eight-ton airplane had just cleared the telephone wires on Genesee Street when it dipped slightly. The small crowd below gasped, but then the Airacuda resumed its climb. The left engine had backfired, blowing open the intercooler, air ducts, and part of the engine cowling. There had been a momentary loss of power; had the engine quit, the Airacuda almost certainly would have crashed.

Lt. Kelsey completed a twenty-five minute flight and brought the aircraft back for repairs. A second flight was made on September 24. Once again, Bell, Whitman, and Woods were on hand, as well as several members of the board of directors.

"Look!" shouted Bell as the Airacuda touched down. "He's in trouble!"

The right strut had failed to lock and the landing gear buckled. The aircraft went into a ground loop, damaging the right wing and the blades of the right propeller. Kelsey was unhurt.

The Airacuda.

The Bell YFM-1 team at the Buffalo airport before a flight to Wright Field, Dayton, Ohio. From left, Art Fornoff, service manager; J. Frederick Schoellkopf IV, pilot/sales manager; Charles Beard, treasurer; Lt. Benjamin Kelsey, army test pilot; Larry Bell, Ray Whitman, and Airacuda designer Bob Woods.

The Airacuda after a crash when the right wheel strut collapsed at Buffalo airport, September 24, 1937.

Repairs were made, and ten successful flights were conducted before the airplane was flown to Wright Field for formal army acceptance on October 21. There were extensive tests; and, the following May, Bell Aircraft received an order for 13 YFM-1 prototype Airacudas.

There were several differences between the XFM-1 and the YFM-1s. The carburetor air scoops were moved down from the tops of the engine nacelles, the superchargers were changed from external to built-in, and the fuselage gun blisters were taken off in favor of flush ports for the mid-fuselage machine guns. Spinners were added to the propeller hubs.

On speaking engagements, Larry embellished the Airacuda legend: "We named it after the barracuda, the tiger fish. It's not a ship for war, but for defense. Too long our designers have worked at bombers. The result is that cities along the seacoast would have been helpless in the event of an attack by air. The United States had nothing capable of staving them off. We saw the need, conceived the plans, presented the idea, then built the ship."

The Airacuda's tricycle landing gear was no instant success. A serious problem of nose wheel shimmy had to be solved, and a long series of trial-and-error tests were conducted to check hydraulic dampers in various positions and various speeds. Some of these tests were conducted by fitting a Bell nose wheel to a test cart. A typical day's effort was a series of nineteen trial runs made on March 8, 1938, on Vicksburg Road, Town of Tonawanda, near the Elmwood plant.

J. Fred Schoellkopf IV reported: "Upon reaching a speed of 15 mph on Elmwood Avenue [headed toward the test site], a violent shimmy developed, which necessitated cutting loose from the tow car. To prevent recurrence in view of the public, an arm was placed in position and snubber was set in fully closed position No. 1.

"Present at testing ground: Fred Schoellkopf, at controls of test cart and in charge of determining program and recording data. Two Bell Aircraft men for traffic control and cart adjustments. One Riverside trucking man for driving tow car, and one insurance man for observation. Dave Forman appeared at 1:30 P.M. with a camera to replace the one damaged day before. . . ." Among the conclusions: "From tests to date we can assume that the use of a hydraulic snubber is necessary and efficient for shimmy control."

First delivery took place on February 23, 1940; and the tenth of the series, designated the YFM-1B, was delivered on July 30, 1940. The final three of the contract were equipped with tricycle landing gear for improved ground handling. They were designated YFM-1A, and all were delivered in October 1940.

At a secret hearing before a House Appropriations Subcommittee in February 1939, General Arnold testified that the Airacuda was an extremely superior combat aircraft. He described the YFM-1 as "the most striking example of airplane development of the last year anywhere in the world." The Airacuda carried a crew of five. It had a wing span of seventy feet and was slightly more than forty-seven feet long. Service ceiling was 25,000 to 35,000 feet. Cruising speed was listed as 220 mph, and top speed, more than 300 mph, although records show 271 mph as the top speed attained by this airplane.

An oddity of the Airacuda was the fact that it could not taxi. The liquid-cooled engines had radiators that relied on the flow of air created by flight. On the ground, the engines could be operated only for a short time before they would overheat. All ground movements of the Airacuda had to be made by tow tractor.

The Airacuda also had the first aircraft auxiliary power unit—a small engine-generator system that, in the XFM-1, provided 110-volt alternating current. Later models had a 24-volt direct current system.

The army stationed its Airacudas at various parts of the country for pilot training and additional modifications. Except for the unit Bell had installed on the Consolidated A-11, Allison engines were new to aviation. Much of the Airacuda development program was directed toward adapting and refining these engines for flight.

Other than its engineering advancements, however, the Airacuda was a dead-end. No more aircraft were ordered, and YFM-1 No. 3 was displayed as a novelty at the 1939 World's Fair. Because of crashes, only nine existed when the United States entered World War II and began mustering its forces. In January 1942, the army ordered all FM-1s to be flown to Chanute Field, Illinois. The big fighter/bomber/bomber-killer never saw combat. The Airacudas spent the rest of their days at Chanute, Keesler, and Lowery Fields.

The nation dropped the effort for a twin-engine, multiplace, long-range escort aircraft, but, later in World War II, airplanes with the general characteristics of the Airacuda proved to be of major tactical importance over Europe. The program gave these innovations to the aviation industry:

—First modern tricycle landing gear.
—First extension drive shaft.
—First hydraulically-dampened 50-caliber machine gun mount.
—First use of remote fire control and ranging mechanisms.
—First use of Allison engines in an airplane designed for them.
—First airborne 37-millimeter cannons. These were fired automatically or manually.

The advanced concepts were costly. By the time the Airacuda production line was underway, the army could buy a conventional B-17 bomber for half the price of an Airacuda. In Larry Bell's mind, the Airacuda was far more than just a favorite first aircraft. It was the source of much of his company's future, and it also combined two things he loved best—engineering beauty and top-quality craftsmanship.

"It was one of the finest airplanes this country's ever had," said Bell near the end of his life. "But it was too early. It was far too advanced for the day and for a requirement that never came to be. And it was too expensive. The price for an Airacuda was $219,000. In those days that was too much."

7

Germany,
Before and After

In mid-summer, 1938, the German liner *Europa* rested at anchor off Southampton, while boats carried cargo and passengers back and forth from shore. Larry moved restlessly along the deck toward the bow, then suddenly ducked down a passageway to the stateroom he shared with Lucille.

He was reading when he heard the drone of unmuffled aircraft engines. Opening a porthole, he murmured, "Sounds like in-lines."

Larry rushed back topside just as the first British bomber swooped up over the bow and crossed the ship no more than ten or twenty feet over the mast. One by one the remaining airplanes in the formation lined up for their runs.

Standing next to Larry were three ship's officers who watched expressionlessly. One gestured and uttered something in German. Larry didn't understand, but he could see what they were talking about. The officer had pointed at the target of the practice bombing raid. It was the one Nazi symbol in sight, a swastika flying from the mast.

A young officer turned to Bell with the expression of a victim of a crime looking at an impartial bystander. "We are witnessing the lion at play," he said in perfect English.

"They're carrying live torpedoes," said Bell. "The lion plays rough."

Larry and Lucille had sailed out of New York on the *Europa* at a minute after midnight, Saturday, July 15, 1938. He was one of a number of U.S. industrialists sent overseas at the request of President Roosevelt, who wanted first-hand information on preparations for war in Europe.

The trip was made despite problems at the plant. Bell Aircraft was still struggling to survive against well-established rivals. At the end of 1937, the company had only a little more than $43,000 net profit. In April, 1938, a new airplane, the XP-39A, had made its first flight. In May, Bell Aircraft had received its first major production contract, for thirteen Airacudas.

In a letter to his brother, Vaughn, he noted two side-effects the trip would have: "I will learn a tremendous amount about European military aviation and enhance my prestige at home."

When the ship docked at Hamburg, Larry and Lucille were met by old air force friends, Major Arthur W. Vanaman, assistant air attache at the American embassy, and Vanaman's wife, Sally. From the moment Larry stepped on German soil, he reported he liked what he saw. The Autobahn was a marvel. Villages were clean and quaint. The people everywhere were friendly.

Larry later recalled that he had come to Germany with the impression that he would encounter "a nation of militant, goose-stepping brutes." What he reported finding were men and women who seemed to share his deep respect for life. In the vestibule of a village restaurant near Berlin, for example, he was touched by the kindness shown for a family of robins which had selected a ceiling light fixture for nesting.

The restaurant owner had disconnected the switch and laid newspapers on the floor to catch droppings from the young family. Everyone who walked by took care not to disturb the baby robins and their parents. It was exactly the kind of thing Larry himself might have done if he had arrived at work one morning and found a bird's nest in his office.

"I had heard all kinds of things about Germany," Bell recalled. "But there was no goose-step swagger in the people I saw in that restaurant."

Riding in the shiny 1937 Ford the Vanamans had brought with them to Germany, the visitors were taken first to the American embassy and then to the German Air Ministry in Berlin. General Ernst Udet and Major Walter Wendtland helped plan a thorough two-week tour of Germany's aircraft industry.

A surprise was in store for Larry. The Germans had arranged

to have George Madelung—a friend from Larry's days at the Glenn L. Martin plant in Cleveland—to accompany the Bells. Dr. Madelung, who headed a large research facility in Stuttgart, was widely known in the German aviation industry and was Willy Messerschmitt's brother-in-law. "It would be worth the whole trip just to spend the time with Professor Madelung!" exclaimed Bell.

The two men had kept in touch after Dr. Madelung left the Martin Company and returned to Germany in the 1920s. In 1937, Dr. Madelung was deeply involved in the Nazi mobilization effort, but wrote the following words to Larry:

". . . I do not think it is quite the right thing. It was much nicer to be a small airplane designer in the G.M.C. [Glenn Martin Co.] in old Cleveland, Ohio. Wasn't it a nice bunch of fellows!"

"I keep those years in my memory as the most satisfactory period of my life. I believe I got spoiled then. Some times in the night I am dreaming I am back in America in the aircraft factory and am altogether happy."

In the same letter he had recalled a remark Larry had made after several days of around-the-clock work: "Do you remember, Bell, how fourteen years ago you said that you did not intend to live more than ten years more?"

Later, on a brief visit to the United States that did not allow a sidetrip to Buffalo, Dr. Madelung wrote that he had considered staying in the United States. "I will, however, not be a deserter," he wrote. "As conditions have developed during the last six weeks, the situation looks quite serious. One cannot resign while every able man's service is required. Maybe I am now under the influence of the New York newspapers, and I shall see matters less darkly when back home. If everything calms down and I find I can leave honorably, I shall let you know."

Larry had never seen anything anywhere that matched the effort Germany was putting into mobilization in 1938. Hitler had tossed aside all restraint in March 1935, when he repudiated the Treaty of Versailles, and in March 1938, when he had ridden into Austria with little more than a whimper for resistance. In September of the same year, at Munich, France, and Great Britain would abandon Czechoslovakia. The myth of Nazi invincibility was making conquest cheap.

Bell and George Madelung were given an especially warm

welcome at the Messerschmitt plant in Augsburg. What impressed Larry most was the contrast between American-style batch production and the mass production assembly lines he saw at Messerschmitt.

Even experimental programs were done on a large scale. Larry was told that as many as two hundred airplanes of a new type would be produced, in order to perfect development through service tests.

At the end of a long line of Me 109s, Larry asked Messerschmitt, "What are all of these for?"

"What is the Airacuda for?" was the reply.

Later, when he was being told the dimensions of an Me-109, Larry interrupted: "That doesn't sound right to me. Do you mind if I tape-measure it?" There was no objection, and Larry and Major Vanaman put a tape measure to Germany's best fighter.

Of the experimental work he saw, Larry was most impressed by the helicopter at Focke-Wulf. First flown in 1936, the FW-61 helicopter had two rotors which turned in opposite directions to offset each other's torque.

That night in his hotel room, Larry wrote words that sounded very much like the things Charles Lindbergh was telling the world in 1938:

"Most impressive is the individual effort, the output, the organization, and the spirit and enthusiasm of the German workers. Production methods are far superior to anything in America or any other country because they are doing things on a large scale that lends itself to progressive production methods. You get the feeling they can do anything."

To get his reports out of Germany, Larry wrote letters addressed to himself and gave them to Major Vanaman, who sent them to Washington in diplomatic pouches. Then they were put in the mail to Buffalo.

Larry frequently took notes and asked for photographs of what he saw. A few years later, Larry's new assembly plant in Niagara Falls was a close copy of one of the ultra-modern facilities he had seen in Germany, probably the Heinkel plant. "As near as I could recall and remember," Bell said after the war, "Bell Aircraft's new plant was a duplicate of that factory— copied right out, because it was the most modern thing I had seen."

Larry gave a brief talk at an Air Ministry luncheon on his last day in Berlin. With Dr. Madelung as the interpreter, he thanked his hosts and praised the progress being made by German industry. "You know that I'll tell my government of what I have seen," said Larry. "That is the purpose of my visit. But although I am traveling other countries, I will not give them this information."

General Ernst Udet then spoke, and Larry later recalled his last words: "Herr Bell, you can give all the information you want to America, and in fact you can tell anybody you want. But we'd rather not that you tell England."

Larry and Lucille spent the weekend with Madelung and his family in Stuttgart and, on Sunday night, boarded a train for Rome. "There's only one airplane I want to see in Italy," Larry said at breakfast served in their car the next morning. "It's the Breda 88, which is supposed to have a top speed of 344 mph."

The couple went sightseeing in Rome, Naples, Capri, and Florence, then visited the Breda plant in Milan. Larry's notes expressed doubt about the high speed Breda aircraft. "I do not think it is as fast as the Messerschmitt 110," he reported.

A high point of the visit to France was a grand night on the town in Paris with a friend, Jack Sterling. French industry, however, was in "pathetic condition," Larry noted. "This is due to political, economic, and labor difficulties. The production is very low, and the morale in the plants lower."

An old friend from Buffalo, Les Irvin of the Irvin Air Chute Company, used his private Stinson to fly the Bells to London for a weekend. A few days later, on his formal visit, Larry toured the British aircraft industry and got the impression that "they cannot possibly reach minimum defense requirements in aircraft for another 12 to 18 months."

He wrote that the British "have some good aircraft but their ability to get into production has been most ineffective. The Spitfire, which is about the same type of airplane as the 109 and about the same age, is still not in production. Confidentially, I saw the sixth Spitfire airplane being completed."

The Bells returned to the United States on the Queen Mary. As soon as they had settled and Larry had checked on progress at the plant, he arranged a trip to Washington to discuss his findings with General Arnold and Assistant Secretary of War Louis A. Johnson. Later, Bell prepared a formal written report to the Navy Department, spelling out in detail his discoveries abroad.

Some of Bell's observations showed weakness in Germany. Larry saw cows hitched with horses to pull plows and knew no farmer would do that unless there was a shortage of horses. And when he asked why farms had geese but not the variety of other birds he remembered in Indiana, Larry was told, "Geese thrive on insects. They don't need much food. We have no food to spare in Germany."

But the official report dated September 12, 1938, stressed Larry's observation that, as far as military aircraft were concerned, Germany was stronger than all the rest of Europe combined. He rated Germany at 10, England at 5, Italy 2, and France 1.

"Potentially, England is stronger than a ratio of 5 but will certainly require at least another year to reach anything that could be considered minimum defense in the air against Germany," Bell reported. "It is more than probable that England's present monthly expenditure on aircraft is much greater than that of Germany."

In two sentences, Larry summed up the situation as it looked in late-summer of 1938: "Germany's present output is certainly not less than 8,000 to 10,000 planes per year. Its efficiency is so high that its aircraft production appears to be smooth and without confusion; the reverse is true in England."

Bell said Italy "is building aircraft less intensively than a year and a half ago, and . . . it is exporting all of the military aircraft it can sell." Of France, he said the status of military aircraft production "appeared to be pathetic in view of the possible need of this equipment. Both Air Ministry officials and aircraft executives were frankly apologetic. . . ."

Bell estimated he saw 20 to 30 percent of Germany's aircraft industry—5.05 million square feet of floor space and 40,000 employees. "On the basis of 25 percent, this would give Germany 20.2 million square feet of floor space and 160,000 employes. This is exclusive of engines, propellers, instruments, accessories, and armament," he reported.

Germany's industry was spread out in small towns and cities, while England and France had large central plants in the large cities. "Each plant [in Germany] consists of many separate buildings separated by at least 1,000 feet. They are so staggered that no three buildings are in line, as a protection against bombardment. . . ."

In his report, Larry wrote a warning for the U.S. government: "Great Britain has apparently made tremendous mistakes in endeavoring to build up its aircraft production during the past few years. It is my strong recommendation that our government examine carefully what has happened in this British effort to get emergency aircraft production if the same mistakes are to be avoided here in the event of a similar emergency."

Larry found that "after two years of failure, England is employing what may be termed a dictatorship with regard to aircraft procurement. Stupendous sums are being spent more or less on a cost plus basis, and it is my judgment that three quarters of British aircraft now on order and in production is without a determined cost price.

"As an example, the Messerschmitt 109 single engine pursuit and British Spitfire are about equal as to performance and general value; both types are nearly two years old. Germany is producing at least five Messerschmitts per day in the Messerschmitt plant and five other plants are in quantity production on this model. More than two thousand Spitfires are on order, and on August 24, 1938, the sixth Spitfire was completed. Lord Nuffield, automobile manufacturer, in July received an order for one thousand Spitfires, and in August ground was broken to begin the building of a factory to manufacture the planes."

A Navy Department summary of the report was sent to President Roosevelt, who most likely saw it as confirmation of what he knew of mobilization in Germany and weakness in the rest of Europe. In any event, at a press conference on October 14, the president announced that he was making an entirely new study of the nation's defense needs as a result of "new information of a technical rather than a political nature."

The president said he was particularly concerned about mass production of war equipment, including airplanes. He said the production question was something new and intimated that one of the phases to be studied was standardization of plane production.

A day earlier, Bernard M. Baruch, who had chaired the War Industries Board, said, "The threat to the United States from Germany is in South America and is real and immediate. Our air forces are not what they should be. We haven't quantity production as in Germany. We ought to produce a minimum quantity of planes for our needs now of proven types and arrange for mass production in an emergency."

The Bell airplane Bell never built: BG-1 dive bomber/scout. The company obtained the license for this airplane and did some experimental work with it.

A distinguished visitor, Charles A. Lindbergh, with Bob Woods, Bob Stanley and Jack Woolams.

Captured German P-1101, the Messerschmitt swing-wing on which the X-5 was patterned.

The Douglas A-20A, a design which Assistant Secretary of War Louis A. Johnson reported was boldly lifted from the Germans by Larry Bell during his 1938 visit.

Larry with General Arnold and William S. Knudsen on September 9, 1940. The government was trying to decide whether Bell Aircraft could handle the kind of production levels anticipated as war raged in Europe.

The first working helicopter, Focke-Wulf's FW-61, which Larry Bell got a chance to see in 1938 as a visitor to Germany.

The quote was underlined in Larry's copy of the *New York Post*. He was swept by a sense of urgency and asked for tireless efforts on the Airacuda and other programs.

In a November 10 memo to executives, Bell wrote, "In view of the terrific amount of work ahead of this organization, for the next few months it is absolutely necessary that all departmental heads and their various assistants report for work promptly at 8:00 A.M. each day and, furthermore, put in as much overtime at night and Saturdays as is necessary to whip our complicated problems. It may be terrifically irritating if any of the department heads are late any morning thereby holding up decisions. Mr. Whitman is requested to keep and submit to me a punctuality chart of executives and key personnel."

A siege was on that would not let up until after the war. Through the conflict, Larry, a life-long Germanophile, often thought of his friends and acquaintances in Germany. The opportunity to find out what had happened to them came while the Nazis were still fighting in the spring of 1945. The air force invited Bob Woods to head a team of engineers in examining Germany's technical left-overs. The Americans went to London on April 27, where they received training in how to survive in a country still at war, with a special course on how to spot booby-traps.

Woods had instructions from Bell to find George Madelung and find out all he could about Messerschmitt, especially its latest aircraft developments. But Woods, instead, was stationed in a castle and sent on tour of bomb-devastated cities.

"So far I have seen quite a lot of London, Strasbourg, Stuttgart, Saarbrücken, Ulm, Augsburg, and Munich," Woods reported on May 8, 1945. "The German cities are really busted up. Our boys do nice neat work, I tell you.

"The Germans are very friendly in general toward the Americans whom they seem to like and respect. They are scared to death of the Russians and don't seem to like the French or British too much. . . ."

Woods' wit showed in his reports. Thousands of miles away, he could feel Larry's rage that Bell's top engineer was not getting a peek at advanced German aircraft designs. "Don't fire me until I get home," he ended one letter to Larry.

Woods described the situation in this manner: "At the present time I am living in a real castle named Seeburg outside Munich. There used to be a Nazi Baroness around here, but she got kicked out. Sunday night she said she was going to shoot herself, but she was back again tonight [Tuesday] for some of her stuff, and no bullet holes were evident. These Nazis are sure full of it."

Bomb damage in Stuttgart particularly impressed Woods: "Bombing is a real menace, as Stuttgart is a wreck, mostly done in one forty-minute raid. If you took Buffalo and blasted partially or completely all buildings from Kenmore to Lacka-wanna [the entire city], it would give you a rough idea. Down-town, there would not be one remaining habitable office or store. Greater Stuttgart was about the size of Buffalo. You wonder as you look at the stuff if it can ever be rebuilt."

On June 1, Larry wrote to Woods, "I am enclosing a clipping from a New York newspaper of recent date regarding jet heli-copters found in Bavaria, date line, Rosenheim, Bavaria. I hope you will make a special effort to investigate this matter."

By the time Woods had received this information, he was at work in Messerschmitt's relocated headquarters at Oberam-mergau. The Augsburg plant Larry had visited in 1938 had been destroyed.

Woods's engineering team found some Germans who had worked in the plant. "They told us whether it was safe to open doors or whether the whole place would be likely to blow up if we touched something," Woods reported.

The Americans sifted through tons of documents and made several discoveries. "So far I have been somewhat disap-pointed in the amount of really new and advanced design im-provements I have seen," Woods wrote to Larry on June 4. "I have seen much that is different, but when the reasons for such design are tracked down it is much the same old stuff. Mach Nos. of 0.9 have not been successfully exceeded by aircraft—and the answer, as to us, is unknown apparently. They worked on many radical ideas and spent a lot of money on very fine and fancy test equipment. The large sweep-back theory, which is still coming out of the mill, may be new and important on the MX-653 [designation for the Bell XS-1 program]."

A few days earlier, Woods had reported that "'the hot boys' [in Germany were] in the middle of a lot of work that is directly applicable to MX-653 and associated projects. Before I come back I should have very good dope on the ME-163 design ideas, the problems of transonic stability and control, and the four German anti-aircraft missiles—which were under development

Bell Aircraft Corporation's first contract: installing an in-line Allison engine in the Consolidated A-11 aircraft. Larry Bell, hatless, is standing second from left.

The Bell test pilots late in World War II: Front row, from left, Joseph Barekman, Robert O'Gorman, Robert F. Morris, Tex Johnston, Harold Dow. Standing, from left, Robert T. Borcherdt, Joseph Cannon, Jay Demming, Arthur W. Nelson, James Waite, Jack Woolams, Floyd Carlson, and Robert Gorrill.

On November 2, 1940, accompanied by Larry Bell, President Roosevelt rides his limousine through the Bell plant. Two employes, John Marmion and Walter Clark, recalled that Larry had a P-39 hurriedly assembled to look complete. "You'd have thought it was ready to fly," they said, "but under the cowling there wasn't any engine."

Augsburg, Germany, in 1938 during the visit of Bell Aircraft president Larry Bell. Overhead flies a Messerschmitt Me 108.

Courtesy Messerschmitt-Bolkow-Blohm

—as well as some other stuff. . . . If what these 'Krauts' say is correct, the MX-653 may need wings and tails the planform of the ME-163 to pass into the compressibility speed range without dangerous change in trim. These boys could be wrong, too, but they insist they are on the beam up to 1,000 kilometers per hour."

What surprised Woods most was that the Germans had been concentrating on guided missiles and high speed aircraft, while the west had concentrated on bomber aircraft.

Larry also made a postwar inspection tour of Germany that year, bearing the USAF rank of colonel, as did chief test-pilot Jack Woolams. Bell joked about it: "After subjecting myself to all those shots [for an aborted trip to Russia] I feel that I ought to take a trip someplace, if only to test their efficiency."

When the company's tenth anniversary arrived on July 10, 1945, Larry was in London. He and helicopter designer Bart Kelley had dinner alone that night in the Strand, and talked so long that Kelley missed the last subway train to the neighborhood where he was staying with his sister.

"Come to the hotel," said Larry. "There's a big couch in my suite." That night he told Kelley, "If you ever start your own company, don't put your name on it. Name it Ajax or something."

"Why's that, Larry?"

"The responsibilities get too heavy," said Bell. He paused and added, "And when your name's out front you have to do a lot of things that are a terrible bore."

On October 24, 1947, Louis A. Johnson, former assistant secretary of war, announced before the Senate War Investigating Committee that Bell had been one of forty-five industrialists who became industrial spies at the request of President Roosevelt in 1938–39. Outside the committee room following his testimony, Johnson told a *Buffalo Evening News* reporter a story that had not been known—that, because of Larry Bell's courage, the United States obtained concepts used in the Douglas A-20 aircraft that was put into action in the early days of the war.

Johnson said the incident happened when Larry was being shown through a plant on the outskirts of Berlin. A canvas shroud covered an aircraft in one building, and the Germans gave no indication of showing what was underneath, so Larry pulled off the canvas himself.

"If anyone else had done it, the Germans would have shot him," said Johnson, noting that two Americans had earlier tried to find out, unsuccessfully, what the aircraft looked like. Larry never completely confirmed or denied this story; however, a friend, L. Welch Pogue, told Larry in 1951 that he had heard Louis Johnson tell the story in detail. Johnson had said that while Air Marshal Goering was showing Bell and other U.S. visitors around one of the factories, Bell "managed to get tangled up" in a canvas that covered a secret project. Larry took the cover off as he untangled himself and calmly inspected the project as the guards hurriedly pulled the cover back on.

Larry's response, made in a letter to Pogue, speaks for itself: "I have heard [Johnson] tell the story on a couple of occasions and while it is obviously true he does embellish it a little bit in spots."

Bob Woods received the President's Medal of Freedom in 1950 for the ingenuity and courage he had displayed in gathering technical information in his late-war trip to Germany. In giving Woods the medal, Major General Laurence C. Craigie said the assignment was "really a military mission fraught with danger."

A number of Germans came to work at Bell following the war. The most prominent was Walter R. Dornberger, former major general and commander of the Peenemunde Rocket Research Institute that produced the V-2 missile used against England and Belgium.

8

A Hot Design
Turns Heavy

In the middle of the desk was a United Auto Workers leaflet handed to Larry by a grim-faced organizer at the gate that morning. "We mean business, Mr. Bell," the heavy-set man had said. All day long, the document sat on Larry's desk. He picked it up several times, studied it, then put it down and went to work on other business.

After work, when the plant had emptied, he walked into Ray Whitman's office with the leaflet in his hand. "Ray, let's waive the representation vote and recognize this outfit. These are the same men who belonged to Consolidated's union," he said.

"They're labor to the core," said Whitman. "Why not get it over without a lot of fuss?"

The first contract with United Auto Workers Local 501 was signed on August 4, 1937. It was a brief document that provided six annual holidays, a forty-hour work week, and time-and-a-half for overtime. Local President E. M. Swartz signed for the union.

There was a section for wage rates, but the space was blank.

The company's stock was selling well as a result of the Airacuda production contract, and the engineers were busy designing two radical new airplanes. Models 3 and 4 were Bell's entries in an Army competition for a high-performance, single-place, single-engine fighter.

Larry was part of the design effort. On one occasion, he praised Woods for "scrounging up a better way of doing the job," saying, "Compare these designs with the P-36 and P-40, which are good conventional airplanes, and you can see what we've got. They carry that pea shooter, the 30 caliber. These have a 20mm cannon and two 50-caliber machine guns. They're faster and have better visibility."

In order to design an airplane around such heavy armament, Bell left space up front for the cannon. A gun that size could not safely be synchronized and fired through the propeller blades, so in Bell's plane it would fire through the hub.

Colonel Oliver P. Echols at Wright Field told Bell that his designs were "the kind of plane the army wants," but urged him to be patient with the slow process of industry-wide competition.

The Bell people worked out a plan to make a movie as a surprise weapon against their competition. The company hired photographers experienced in making training films, and Bell called a meeting with them to make the requirements clear. "There are several important, unique features that need to be shown," said Bell, standing in front of a wall on which drawings of Models 3 and 4 were taped. "In both designs the engine has been moved back from the nose. That means the heaviest element of the airplane has been placed close to the center of gravity with consequent increased maneuverability.

"In the case of the Model 4, this permits a sleek streamlined nose offering far less drag than the conventional blunt cowling, with consequent additional speed. The 'empty' nose allows installation of a cannon bigger than anything being flown today— as well as a nose wheel that makes this airplane the only single engine fighter that can have a tricycle landing gear. These are very important assets. Finally, take note that in the Model 4 the pilot will be seated *in front* of the leading edge of the wing, with enormously increased visibility."

A photographer interrupted, "Mr. Bell, we can't really show these things without animation of some kind. It might be best for us to film your talk, with drawings, just like you've given it today."

"No," Larry replied. "Their idea is to judge the document and not be influenced by anybody's sales pitch, on film or off. We'll film the full-scale mock-ups of these planes. You've got to make a documentary film that simply relates the important features of each aircraft. Of course, it will contain some salesmanship but not a direct sales pitch."

The completed film was viewed by Bell, Woods, and Whitman

Early production Airacobras of the type that saw service with the U.S. forces in the South Pacific.

Tailhook version of the P-39, the XFL-1 Airabonita.

This is the XP-39A on December 3, 1938, before it was given the designation P-39. "Bell Model 3" was undergoing ground tests when this photograph was taken.

A mockup of Bell Model 3, the design which placed the engine in front of the pilot. It lost out to Bell Model 4 (which became the P-39), but some of its characteristics were used by Bob Woods in the design of the later XP-77.

The P-39 power system put the engine behind the pilot and the drive shaft under his seat and between his legs. Above, the power system photo illustrates the space available for the cannon behind the gearbox in the nose. The cannon fired through the propeller shaft.

J. Fred Schoellkopf IV after a P-39 test flight.

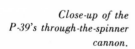

Close-up of the P-39's through-the-spinner cannon.

in the studio downtown. "This may be the first movie ever made for one showing before an audience of seven," said Bell as they walked out into daylight.

"We've got what that audience is looking for," said Woods.

The thirty-minute film was submitted with the drawings and specifications that made up Bell's proposal. Several weeks later, the result was telephoned from Wright Field: Model 4 was the winner; Model 3 came in second. The competition hadn't even come close.

The company was instructed to come up with a detailed design of the Model 4 before final go-ahead on building one prototype aircraft. The designation XP-39 was given to the airplane. The original design was destined to be vastly changed before it would be built and then undergo thousands of additional changes throughout its years of service.

The XP-39A contained some of the world's most advanced design features at a weight cost of only 50.7 pounds. That included 40 pounds for a 10-foot drive shaft from the engine to the propeller, and 10.7 pounds for a shaft bearing.

The turbo-supercharged XP-39A was first flown by dive bomber pilot Lieutenant James Taylor (USNR) on April 6, 1938—Air Force Day—at Wright Field. Bell's John L. (Mickey) McCarthy was crew chief. The original airplane was an extremely advanced high-performance machine that had what it took to become the greatest fighter of World War II. But from the beginning, the airplane underwent changes and additions that steadily reduced performance. The P-39 got heavier without additional horsepower to haul the extra weight.

The original aircraft weighed close to 4,000 pounds, could climb to 20,000 feet in five minutes, and could fly at just under 400 miles per hour. By the time a later version, the P-39D, was in production in 1942, the airplane weighed nearly 5,600 pounds. It was capable of good performance only to 10,000 feet.

Weight increases were unavoidable. Wartime technology brought installation of heavy, self-sealing fuel tanks. Armor was added to protect the pilot and vital engine parts. The proposal for a 20-millimeter cannon gave way to a 37-millimeter cannon, and other armament increases further added to the P-39's weight.

The P-39 was to win fame as a ground-support aircraft. Its cannon could destroy tanks, railroad trains, or seagoing ships.

In addition, the airplane had bomb racks and two 50-caliber and four 30-caliber machine guns. The fuselage was extremely rigid to hold the drive shaft in line and could absorb a large amount of battle damage. The tricycle landing gear allowed pilots to land safely on unpaved roads or muddy fields.

Financial problems haunted the company in early 1940 despite the strong possibility of P-39 production awards. Bell Aircraft was losing money on the Airacuda program and breaking even on its work for Consolidated Aircraft.

The financial situation produced some strain on Larry Bell's relationship with treasurer Chuck Beard. At a meeting one Monday morning, Fred Schoellkopf, Bell, Ray Whitman, and Beard discussed the problem.

"It boils down to this," said Beard. "At the present time, the company is just not solvent. We're going broke, and I'm not going to sign any more financial statements."

"That's your job, isn't it?" asked Bell. Beard nodded. "I can't afford to have a treasurer that won't go along with me. What is it you need?"

"We need more business," said Beard. "We're going out of business, and we need somebody who is willing to make an advance payment."

Bell went to New York that night to meet Sir Henry Self at the Anglo-French Purchasing Board, 15 Broad Street. The topic was a possible contract from France for the P-400 (export version of the P-39 modified to European specifications). At the time, in April 1940, Britain was handling France's military purchases in the United States.

When Bell entered the British offices, Self's secretary stayed at his side and pulled up a chair next to him as he sat down. The young lady flipped open a shorthand book and prepared to take notes. Bell looked darkly at Self: "Is she going to take down every word I say?"

"Just a business procedure," said Sir Henry. "Take no notice."

Bell was insulted but said nothing. By the end of the week, he had a $9 million order to build two hundred P-400s for the French. The deal included a $2 million advance, and when Bell got on the train for Buffalo, he had a banknote for that sum with him.

"You said you wouldn't sign any more financial statements," he told Beard when he handed him the banknote the next morn-

ing. "I'll sign them from here on out." Beard survived the
incident, but Bell had come close to firing one of the men who
had helped start the company. Years later in the company
magazine *Bellringer*, Beard described the problems of being
treasurer in a company that often had held its breath each
payday: "It's a mighty hard thing to meet a payroll of a little
less than a hundred employees when the only book ever opened
was labeled "Accounts Payable." Very often, I would figure for
hours on how to meet the payroll before I'd be forced to bother
Larry Bell, who always came through. Even though the money
was scarce, payless paydays never happened at Bell."

Office furniture was also scarce in the early years; and, if an
employee wound up with a chair that had flat wheels, he was
stuck with it. Not content with the status quo, timekeeper Herb
Sommer came in early one morning, pushed his battered chair
down the darkened hall, and switched for a later model whose
owner was still home in bed. Just as he made the change,
Sommer heard a knuckle rap on the corridor window. He
looked up and was startled to see Larry Bell looking at him.
"Early bird get the worm?" asked Bell with a smile.

The $2 million advance on the French contract took the pain
out of Bell's losses on the Airacudas. But he had to explain the
problem at a directors' meeting. Bell said that the Army was
being "very meticulous. They're not going to allow any more
than actual costs with a 45 percent overhead." Rolling up his
prepared report into a pipe, he said, "That's inadequate, and it
means we're going to have to pay for flight testing from company funds."

After some questioning, Bell explained that the army held to
its policy of paying no more overhead than the company was
running on its other current contracts. At the time, that meant
subcontracting the PBY wing panels. "As far as profits are
concerned, we can write off the Airacuda," said Bell. "But that
airplane has assured our future."

There was only one production P-39 in existence on January
6, 1940, when Captain George E. Price of the Army Air Corps
demonstrated the first assembly-line aircraft before a large
group of military visitors gathered in a wooden hangar at
Buffalo Airport. Bell couldn't have been more pleased at the
pilot's skill. Price flew low over the flat field at more than 300
miles per hour, swinging the plane up at a steep angle over
Genesee Street and then performing an Immelmann backflip

turn to "attack" the hangar where the visitors were sheltered from the cold.

The P-39's Allison engine whined a smooth, efficient roar; and the airplane's 37mm cannon jutted like a battering ram through the spinner. The generals got an enemy's-eye view of the P-39 that was enough to make them shudder.

Captain Price pulled a circling climb over the airport to demonstrate altitude capabilities, then made a steep power dive. It was a perfect final act—a tiny speck that grew to an intimidating whirlwind of howling air and the high-pitched whine of twelve unmuffled cylinders. There was applause as Captain Price made a final pass for the landing. Bell, Whitman, and Bob Woods shook hands, grinning.

But the P-39 was acting strangely. It didn't land. Instead, it headed out toward an unpopulated part of the suburb, slowly gaining altitude. Bell walked swiftly to the control tower. Once inside the door, he ran up the steps and asked the controller if he was in contact with Captain Price.

"He can't get the gear down," said the controller. "Do you want to talk to him?"

Larry was out of breath and sweating as he moved around the counter to the microphone. "George Price," he said. "Have you tried the emergency handcrank?"

The pilot explained he had gone from manual to electric drive several times, but that the mechanism was jammed.

By this time, crew chief Mickey McCarthy was at Bell's side. "That could be it," he said. "It's slushy down here on the field, but below freezing aloft."

"Dammit, Mickey; why didn't we foresee this?" said Bell, as he turned to the microphone. "Captain Price," he said, "I'm ordering you to head that airplane toward the lake and bail out."

"Negative, Mr. Bell," said Price. "I don't think it's as bad as that."

"Let me remind you, this is a Bell company demonstration," Larry said. "That aircraft has yet to be proven. You get out now."

"I've thought of something," said the voice in the speaker.

As the crowd watched silently, Captain Price brought the P-39 in for a smooth, slow, wheels-up, belly landing.

"He's demonstrated how tough this airplane is!" said Bell as the P-39 came to a halt. The landing had bent the propeller blades and rubbed off some of the underside skin from the wing and fuselage, but otherwise the P-39 was undamaged.

Thirteen days later, Captain Price demonstrated the same airplane at Bolling Field, Washington, D. C., and later received the Distinguished Flying Cross for bravery in saving the aircraft in Buffalo.

The engineers discovered that ice had not caused the landing gear to fail. A worm gear in the main drive system had locked. An intensive search was made, and it was discovered within a few weeks that the plating on the worm and gear picked up, causing them to bind. The problem was eliminated.

France fell in June 1940, two months after it had placed its order for two hundred Airacobras. Bell immediately returned to the British mission in New York. His company had just started adding men and equipment at the Elmwood plant to carry out the French order. What should he do? "England might need these aircraft itself," Bell said at a meeting with the British. "Up to an altitude of 16,000 feet where it is designed to fight, the Airacobra's performance surpasses that of the Spitfire, the ME 109s, or the Focke-Wulf 190s."

The British took over the French contract and, as Europe collapsed, there was increasing pressure in the United States to bolster U.S. defense. The Airacobra was suddenly looked upon as an ideal national defense weapon—a flying cannon capable of destroying invading bomber squadrons that might rise up out of the horrors underway in Europe.

Bell Aircraft needed more space to get the P-400 production line moving as swiftly as possible. In September 1940, the U.S. Army Air Corps issued Emergency Facilities Contract No. 1, authorizing the company to build a manufacturing plant on a rural sixty-five-acre field adjacent to Niagara Falls Airport north of Buffalo.

The production line of YFM-1 Airacudas was shutting down, and these aircraft were being flown out of Buffalo to various army air fields. In 1940, Bell Aircraft completed the Airacuda project and built two Airacobras. In 1941, Bell built 756 Airacobras.

A combination of research and showmanship brought international attention to the P-39. At the very moment Bell was engaged in negotiations for a major production order for the army, the company decided to try to set a world speed record with the P-39.

On the morning of January 8, 1941, Andrew C. McDonough, a reserve navy lieutenant, took a P-39 to 27,000 feet and made a 21,000-foot power dive. Instruments on the airplane recorded a top speed of 620 mph.

News reports claimed the Airacuda had flown faster than anything recorded before, but there was an aura of publicity stunt in the achievement. At the Elmwood plant, chief test pilot Bob Stanley defended the test as necessary "to guarantee the utmost of safety and reliability of the product under all conditions to be encountered under the stringent requirements of total war."

The army's decision to go into P-39 production was not to be made without intensive advance review by General Arnold's staff. The clincher came during a three-day visit by William S. Knudsen, the head of General Motors Corporation, who had been called into service by President Roosevelt as a member of the advisory committee of the National Defense Commission. Knudsen was the nation's top authority on production. Larry Bell knew he would have to convince Knudsen of the company's production capability or lose the chance for large orders for the Airacobra.

Knudsen's visit was the final test. The president's envoy had come to town to make sure Bell Aircraft was capable of building five airplanes a day. At meetings in Bell's office, and during walks through the plant, Knudsen mentioned this production goal several times. Bell assured him that the young company could meet the goal.

"Well, now, Larry," said Knudsen at the end of the third day, "I have just one more question. How many airplanes have you built, all told?"

"Hundreds of them," said Bell.

"More hundreds than the Martin company? More than Consolidated?"

"I'm one of the most experienced men in the industry," said Bell. "I've built lots of airplanes."

"Yes. But how many airplanes has Bell Aircraft made?"

Bell started to reply, hesitated, then grinned. "You've trapped me. The truth is, this company has built fifteen airplanes since it was started," he said.

"Fifteen airplanes in six years, and you're calmly talking about producing five a day!" said Knudsen, raising his bushy eyebrows.

Knudsen left town without indicating his decision, but on August 25, 1941, Bell Aircraft was notified that it had been awarded a $75 million contract to build 2,000 P-39s for the army. It was the beginning of an expansion program that would spiral practically until the end of World War II. And P-39 production eventually reached twenty airplanes a day.

The first buildings at the Niagara Falls airport plant boosted the company's floor space from 474,262 at the end of 1940 to more than a million square feet a year later. Contractors worked through the winter to get the job done, and the first hundred employes moved into the facility on May 18. Bell had frequently visited the new plant while it was being built, bringing one or two assistants with him each time. On one visit, Bell was inspecting a new building, when a doorknob came off in his hand. He put it back on and asked Edward Paul to make sure it was fixed. It was one of several directives given to Paul that day, and he concentrated on the most important ones first. Paul forgot the doorknob. Several weeks later, Larry suddenly asked Paul if it had been fixed. Paul nodded, hopefully. Without a word, Bell reached into his desk, brought out the doorknob, and handed it to him.

Another close associate of Bell at this time was his older brother, Vaughn, who resigned from a twenty-five-year career in the department store business to come to Bell Aircraft as industrial relations manager in October 1940. Vaughn had at one time been in charge of personnel for a chain of eight stores in Los Angeles.

Aircraft built at the Elmwood plant were trucked north and then assembled and test flown at Niagara Falls Airport. Each aircraft had to meet army acceptance requirements which included a number of ground checks and a full hour and a half of test flying.

Homer Berry—an old-time pilot who flew "by the seat of his pants"—had been Bell Aircraft's first company test pilot. He joined Bell on March 27, 1939, and conducted many of the early Airacobra test flights at the Buffalo airport, where Bell's first experimental flight test hangar was located.

Another pilot, Bryan Sparks, joined Bell in early 1940; but, on June 21 of that year, he was disabled by leg fractures when he parachuted out of a troubled Airacuda. Copilot Jack Strickler rode the airplane to a crash landing on a farm field and was unhurt, but Sparks was not able to return to work until after the

Soviet pilots pose with a much-decorated Airacobra.

Larry and Lucille show Mrs. Roosevelt through the Buffalo plant on April 17, 1941. At Larry's right is assistant Dave Forman.

King Peter of Yugoslavia with the Bells in Buffalo on July 2, 1942.

Tex Johnston with Thompson Trophy and Allegheny Ludlum Award after winning the 1946 Cleveland Air Races.

Jack Woolams, left, and Tex Johnston with Cobras I and II. Woolams died in Cobra I when its windshield collapsed on a high-speed test flight. Johnston went on to win the 1946 Cleveland Air Races in Cobra II.

start of World War II, when he helped in development of the
XP-59A. The wrecked Airacuda was given to Buffalo's Burgard
High School.

There is an intersection just west of the Niagara Falls airport
known as Six Corners that should bear a plaque in memory of
the pilots who performed functional flight tests of production
P-39s. It was over this site that they experienced the excruciat-
ing puckering sensation that accompanies the first seconds off
the ground in a factory-fresh, never-flown airplane.

Richard N. Krashel died at Six Corners in May 1943 when
the engine on his P-39 failed and he tried to bail out. Other test
pilots who died near the airfield were Norman W. Swenson,
December 7, 1942, Clarence Sengpiel, March 21, 1943, and
Aeros Owen, July 21, 1944.

In December of 1944, a combination of bad weather and nose
wheel failure produced some anxious moments for test pilot
Robert Morris. While he worked feverishly at the nose wheel
problem, the weather closed in at Niagara Falls. There was
some thought of abandoning the aircraft, which was not
equipped for instrument landing, but Morris was eventually
talked down to a safe two-point landing by test pilot Jack
Woolams.

Larry Bell's blunt form of leadership was displayed frequently during the company's early period of expansion. In a
May 1941 notice to employes in which he sought support for the
Joint Charities and Community Fund Campaign, he said, "We
wish to make it clear that no pressure will be put on ANY
employe for a contribution. However, we are very definitely in
sympathy with this cause and hope that every Bell worker will
be a real BELL RINGER. . . ." The key word was "however."

As the plants added manpower, Bell concentrated on his
promise to William Knudsen that the company would be able to
produce five Airacobras a day. A new system of coordinated
lofting was devised to replace the traditional method of manufacturing airplanes like custom automobiles.

Flat metal templates were made for practically every P-39
structure, and static production was replaced by a moving assembly line. Each P-39 part was designed to be interchangeable, and aircraft that reached the airport end of the Niagara
Falls plant were ready to be rolled out the door for ground
checkout and first flight.

Ray Whitman was in his office on Sunday, December 7,

1941, when someone rushed in with the news of the Japanese attack on Pearl Harbor. Whitman called Bell and then made arrangements necessary to redesignate a shipment of Britain's completed, crated, P-400s for use by the U.S. Army Air Corps.

Bell and Whitman stood in grim silence the next morning as they watched squads of youthful army troops carrying rifles with bayonets surround the Elmwood plant to guard against saboteurs.

9

The War
Years

Some of the larger aircraft companies expanded one or two times to meet World War II production demands. At Bell Aircraft, expansion was phenomenal. In January 1940, Bell had 1,170 employes. At its wartime peak in February 1944, Bell had increased forty-three times, to 50,674.

By midsummer of 1942, Bell was adding a thousand new employes a week, which posed some unique problems. Trained supervisors were scarce; and, despite production problems that were at their peak in Buffalo, engineers and supervisors had to be uprooted and assigned to the new Georgia Division, or to the Ordnance Division, which moved from Buffalo to Burlington, Vermont, in August 1943.

In 1942, Bell opened a second-shift employment office. Recruiters were there as late as ten-thirty or eleven at night if anyone had an inkling to try a hand at building "Airacobras for Victory." In 1943, Bell built a "Cape-Cod cottage" in Buffalo's downtown business section. Hundreds of office workers were lured to Bell through patriotic rallies, bond drives, and other promotions conducted from this employment corner in disguise.

To have a job at Bell during the war was to be part of an important cause. There were constant changes and an endless flow of new faces and challenges. Since many employes were working overtime as much as seven days a week, the company helped fight boredom by providing newsreel theaters, recreation societies, and frequent rallies and gatherings at which the

103

employes, themselves, did the entertaining. Men and women of the third shift formed clubs and went to the local YMCA after work for games and dancing before going home.

From the company's point of view, anything that would help cut down the high rate of absenteeism and labor turnover was worth a try. The monthly magazine, *Bellringer*, and weekly newspaper, *Bell News*, were filled with news about employes' activities and the importance of their jobs.

The high percentage of women at the Niagara Frontier Division led to a number of marriages and other intimate relationships between men and women thrown together for long hours in the vast assembly plants. There is a catwalk leading to a remote platform high in the rafters of the Niagara Falls facility that was still pointed to thirty years later in nostalgic awe for the intense romance of days gone by. And several P-39s left the plant bearing tiny him-and-her initials hidden in the cockpit, although these may have been more wishful thinking than scorekeeping.

One production worker recalled these days as the most exciting in his life. "What a wonderful place to work," he said. "Nobody pushed you too hard, and there were girls all around." He said the open walkway on the South Mezzanine, about ten feet above the production floor, was the object of a great deal of attention. "During breaks, girls would line up and twist their legs through the railing." Later, management had a plywood cover put on that railing!

The company invented "Boypower" in the summer of 1943 to fill gaps on the production line. Bright young high school students were brought in and took to the work rapidly. In the fall, "Double Duty Boypower" was devised. This let boys go to school and also work twenty-four hours a week part time. More than twelve hundred Buffalo area boys participated.

There was also the "Victory Shift" in which bankers, school teachers, clerks, and merchants got a chance to work part time in the war effort. The idea was that a full six-day position on the production line or the machine shop could be filled by two Victory Shifters, each working three consecutive days on the second shift. In the daytime, they worked their regular jobs in other plants.

Larry decided he was wasting too much time driving back and forth from work, so he had a fold-out bed installed in his office and sometimes roamed the plant twenty-four hours a day. It was not unusual for him to phone his assistant, Dave Forman, at 4:00 A.M. and ask, "I didn't wake you up, did I?"

The pressure was relentless. In late 1942, Larry wrote to a doctor at Mayo Clinic, where he had been treated for ulcers: "I am still doing all right—still no smoking, coffee, or tea. Have had a few weak highballs. It seems that if I make them plenty weak they work out all right. I don't think I have ever worked harder or longer hours than I did the past month and am holding my own, but occasionally I have to relax when I feel things aren't just right."

The need for space and employes became so great in early 1943 that Bell made a national search to find a new location for the Ordnance Division and came up with the old Queen City Cotton Mills plant in Burlington, Vermont. The move was made with only a brief lag in production. Buffalo sent 589 employes to Vermont, and in a month, 1,610 employes were on the job at the new plant. Employment for the division reached a peak of 2,538 in June, 1944.

The first sizable gun mount contract had come from the British in 1940, when single and twin 303-caliber mounts were needed for British aircraft being manufactured in the United States. The division also designed a 50-caliber mount for U.S. Navy PT boats and an anti-aircraft mount that was successfully tested on the battleship *Utah*. This led to the Mark 5 gun mount which the navy purchased by the thousands.

When it was in Buffalo, the Ordnance Division won the "Army-Navy E" for production excellence early in the war. Larry decided to use the occasion for a massive open house. Standing on a big banner-covered platform, Larry accepted the award and then thanked the workers who did the job. A band playing the national anthem finished the program. Exactly on the final note, three P-39s roared low over the crowd and climbed straight up into a perfect fleur-de-lis pattern.

It was a dramatic show that brought tears to some eyes. No one would forget the thrill of the moment those P-39s joined the final note of the "Star Spangled Banner."

By the end of the war, the Ordnance Division had produced 104 types of mounts for a wide range of French, British, Russian, and U.S. fighting craft. As the need for gun mounts declined, the division manufactured B-29 parts and made equipment and shells for the Chemical Warfare Service. The gun mount idea that had solved a problem in Airacuda design in

1938 ended up bringing a total of $66 million in business from 1940–45.

The last P-39 rolled off the assembly line on July 24, 1944, ending production of 9,588 of these aircraft. On August 1, the P-63 was announced; and late that year, the *Bell News* noted that Brigadier General Anthony C. McAuliffe, the man who told the Nazis "nuts" at Bastogne, was the brother-in-law of Ray Whitman. Bell began receiving honors for its wartime performance, and Larry was named head of the National Aircraft War Production Council.

Looking toward the future, Bell helped organize the Air Power League, a civilian organization aimed at keeping a permanently strong U.S. air power. But there was a note of farewell in the huge family day open houses held at the divisions in 1944. There were wild rumors that big layoffs were coming soon.

Ray Whitman, who had become manager of the Niagara Frontier Division, as well as first vice president, countered the rumors by writing a "Straight from the Shoulder" column in *Bell News*: "Continue to hit the ball harder than ever to win this war," said Whitman. "Quit worrying. I will keep you informed as far as I am permitted to do so—and above all, don't help Hitler and Hirohito by spreading rumors."

Camp Cataract, the training center for army mechanics which had been founded in an old Niagara Falls hotel, had moved to new barracks near the Niagara Falls plant and was renamed Camp Bell. By the time it closed on November 2, 1944, Camp Bell had graduated a total of 7,432 P-39 and P-63 mechanics.

Bell's motion picture branch had become one of the best in the industry. In addition to its research, maintenance, and training films, the branch produced "It's Your War, Too," a film that originally was designed to interest women in war work but became popular in western New York theaters.

The first aid station was staffed around the clock, so its attendants got to see Larry frequently. One quiet night on the second shift, nurse Mildred George kept herself busy checking supplies. Larry Bell suddenly walked in. "How's it going in here?" he asked with a smile. "Very quiet, Mr. Bell," said Miss George.

He talked to her for a few moments, describing progress in the current war bond drive, then suddenly said, "I don't see

Some of the pilots who ferried Soviet fighters north from the Bell plant. A number of women pilots volunteered for this service.

The Bob Hope Show being broadcast from the Bell bomber plant.

anything here for you to read." "We're not allowed to read on duty," she replied. He shrugged and walked out, with a wave of his hand as he turned the corner.

Three nights later, Larry walked back in and handed the nurse a large stack of brand new magazines. "These are for you," he said. "If anyone asks what you're doing, say you're reading them for me."

The Bell Modification Center became a complete factory in itself at the Niagara Falls plant. P-39s for the northern route to Russia were fitted with a special rapid-service oil drain cock that let crewmen drain the oil before sub-zero cold congealed it. Special radios, cameras, and equipment needed for various missions were installed in other aircraft, such as the P-40 Warhawk and the Beechcraft C-45 transport.

A large batch of P-51B Mustangs was equipped with extra large fuel tanks, and later the employes who worked on them recognized the same aircraft in the war newsreels. The special P-51s were being used in long range fighter protection of U.S. bombers over Germany.

A group of 32 DeHavilland Mosquitoes was equipped with radios and special cameras, but the biggest aircraft to come through for modification was the PBY Catalina Flying Boat. Late in the war, a familiar sight on the parking ramps was a PBY with its 104-foot wing spread over, and shading, a few P-63s that were also being modified. The center handled seven thousand aircraft before the end of the war.

A special set of versatile techniques and skills had been developed by the modification center. Larry Bell knew this unit could be useful after the war when the country seemed likely to modify military equipment to civilian needs. He saw strength also in the helicopter effort and advanced aircraft concepts, but most of all the future depended on the proven capability of the company's engineering force.

During the war, a large number of engineers were concentrated in a giant room on the second floor of the administration building at Niagara Falls. Bell's office was just around the corner. The engineers became accustomed to seeing Larry, alone or with a guest, standing at the head of the room and then walking through rows of men working at drafting boards.

"These are the best engineers in the world," Bell would tell a guest. "There's no problem they can't solve. Nothing they can't get done."

It was a Bell custom for several key executives to have lunch with Larry in the executive dining room. Each working day at 1:00 P.M., Larry presided over a long table where his top managers gathered. Elsewhere in the dining room, separated by a partition, lesser executives lunched.

There was nothing casual about lunch with Larry Bell. He had endless questions and once hounded a vice president, Roy Sandstrom, until the man became speechless—benumbed by Larry's insistent "Tell me what's really going on."

On another occasion, Larry handed out a small mimeographed "test" as coffee was being served. The group was asked to write travel instructions airport-to-Bell for a visiting customer. "Include the numbers for the road in front of this plant," said the instructions.

As he checked the results, Larry shook his head in disbelief. Not a man had remembered both highway numbers. Francis W. Dunn, public relations director, had remembered "State 18," and manufacturing vice president Julius J. Domonkos had written "U.S. 62."

"Astounding," said Bell. "You top salesmen of this company don't even know where headquarters is located!"

The daily challenge at lunch became too much for the executives. The crowd around the long table diminished, and the day finally arrived when Larry had lunch all by himself. A memo to all concerned soon notified the executives that, unless they were out of town, they would eat at 1:00 P.M., no sooner and no later.

In the late war years, Bell looked ahead by dusting off sales techniques that had been set aside for the duration. Once the three products had been established—fighters, bombers, and gun mounts—Larry's powers of persuasion were needed for getting the job done. It had been a tremendous challenge but not the same as selling.

"There's going to be a lot of salesmanship needed after the war," Bell told Ed Paul one afternoon. "In 1940, we produced about 200,000 pounds of airframes. This year, we'll produce more than 30 million pounds. When the war ends, we will suddenly be back to less than the 1940 figure. It's going to take some ingenuity to keep this company going."

Bell paused as Paul remained silent.

"Ed, we learned a lot about the need for salesmanship and promotion from the days with Lincoln Beachey—the greatest pilot in the world. You know my brother, Grover, was part of Beachey's flying team?"

Paul nodded.

"They were all under the management of Bill Pickens, a first class promoter. If Pickens decided to promote a show, he went all out. He spent money. When Pickens came to town to promote Beachey—the headliner, he covered every signboard he could find with pictures of Beachey in his death dive or flying upside down: The *great* Lincoln Beachey.

"It cost a lot of money. I was a mechanic; and one day I asked Pickens, 'What's the idea of you spending so much to advertise Beachey? Everybody already knows Beachey, or ought to.' 'You mean, a fool, like everybody else,' said Pickens, who had the face and disposition of a carnival roustabout. 'My business is to get people in the gate. That's where we get the money.

"'We get them in the gate by advertising before the show. The only reason Beachey shows up at all is otherwise we'd get sued and have to give the money back. We get people to come through the gate. Then Beachey satisfies them. And then they don't sue me.'"

Bell added: "The point is, in Beachey's mind, he was the headliner. The best pilot in the world. And I think he was. But in the mind of his promoter, Beachey was a product. Something unusual that had sales appeal. Something you advertised, produced, and then made sure the customer was satisfied. Everything's got to have a promoter or it gets left on the shelf."

The first rescue mission by a Bell helicopter took place on January 5, 1945, when one of the experimental helicopters still under development was flown from the Gardenville shop to a farmhouse near Lockport, about thirty miles north. The mission had all the elements of every helicopter rescue since.

Instead of waiting for the doctor to drive to Gardenville, the helicopter met him halfway. Plant physician Dr. Thomas C. Marriott drove to a Transit Road parking lot where Floyd Carlson had just landed. Then they were off to rescue chief test pilot Jack Woolams, who had bailed out of a troubled P-59. Test pilot Joe Mashman had been flying a P-59 with Woolams and radioed directions to the helicopter. Heavy snow blocked access to the area by road.

Woolams had hobbled a mile and a half without shoes, which had been pulled off by the inertia of motion when his parachute opened. His feet were badly frozen, and his head was bleeding from a blow suffered when he struggled to get out of the P-59 cockpit. If he had not been helped quickly, Woolams might have suffered permanent injury. As it was, Dr. Marriott was helping him within a few hours after his accident. "My brief trip was only my third airplane ride," the doctor said afterwards. "But I can see where it can be invaluable in situations like the one which confronted us. When Floyd Carlson landed us on Transit Road, it was only a few minutes before I was wading through the deep snow of the farm yard to help Woolams."

Larry Bell had personally ordered the use of the still experimental helicopter. "It's obvious from this experience that helicopters are going to be useful in mercy missions to remote places," said Bell.

The Woolams episode was the first of a long string of rescues—several from the brink of Niagara Falls. They couldn't have been more dramatic if they had been staged, and they served to promote Bell helicopters through newspaper and magazine articles.

In 1944, Bell received the Daniel Guggenheim Medal from the Institute of Aeronautical Sciences, American Society of Mechanical Engineers, and the Society of Automotive Engineers. In accepting the award for achievement in advancement in aeronautics, Larry showed a life-long trait. He couldn't keep quiet about the areas in which his company was doing pioneering work: "Today we are on the threshold of developments in aviation that will accomplish performances undreamed of a few years ago. We may expect the future to perfect radio-controlled missiles of increasing importance in war and a real effort to build airplanes of supersonic speeds."

At that time, Bob Woods was designing the Bell XS-1, the airplane that would be the first three years later to fly faster than sound, and the engineers and test pilots were doing pioneering work in radio-controlled flight.

But in the meantime, a warm welcome awaited Larry Bell in Moscow. He had been personally invited to visit the Soviet Union by Josef Stalin. Several Bell technical representatives had made a trip to Moscow in late 1943 and returned with reports of the importance of the P-39 to Russia's ground war. With so many of his airplanes involved, a visit by Bell seemed to be a logical follow-up.

XS-1 departs from B-29 mother ship.

XS-1 in the loading pit before being raised to meet the bomb-rack-type holders on the B-29.

Jack Woolams, who might have been the first supersonic man if he had not crashed in the Bell racer, Cobra I, on August 30, 1946. XS-1 flight testing was turned over to Chalmers "Slick" Goodlin, who reportedly turned down a $150,000 bonus to attack the sound barrier. The job was given to air force Capt. Yeager, who was making $511.50 a month, including flight pay and extras.

Police rescues dramatized the helicopter and greatly helped its promotion in the early years.

A tremendous amount of effort went into the proposed Russian trip. Through Soviet representatives in the United States, it was learned that it would be appropriate for Larry to bring Marshal Stalin "three fine pipes, a large pipe lighter, and a quantity of tobacco"; for Commissar Mikoyan, a gold pen and pencil set; and for Colonel General Repin and Major General Semichasnov, the newly developed U.S. electric razors. There were to be many lesser gifts for other, less important Communists.

There were problems of insurance, clothing, money, technical movies, and calling cards printed in Russian, and clearances had to be obtained for such sensitive subjects as the first American jet, the P-59. The Russians also wanted information on American machine tools. Larry wanted information on possible postwar sales to the USSR. And the U.S. Air Force wanted information on how the P-63s were performing for the Russians. Larry was told to try to get to a combat area for a look. "What are they using the P-63s for?" General Echols asked.

The trip was to be made on the northern route followed by the P-39s and P-63s, with the takeoff from Washington, D. C., in a C-54, set for May 6, 1945. Informed of the final plan, Major General S. A. Piskounov was reported as "pleased and agreeable, and jokingly suggested that the C-54 be left in Russia."

The war in Europe was ending as the trip plans were finalized. German armies began surrendering May 4, and unconditional surrender was signed on May 7. Suddenly, a visit by a U.S. manufacturer who had provided more than seven thousand airplanes seemed superfluous to Marshal Stalin. The visas didn't arrive as promised, and Larry called a halt to visit plans.

One trip Bell was able to take in 1943 was a ride in a P-39. The engineers had designed a two-place trainer, the TP-39, which had a second cockpit and controls in front of the regular pilot's cockpit. Woods, Whitman, Bell, and Beard took rides in this aircraft. Bob Stanley had an especially wild look in his eye when he took Larry up, and it was a pale and shaken company founder who was helped out of the cockpit twenty minutes later. "Great airplane," whispered Bell, heading for the nearest rest room.

In the late months of the war, the P-63 was selected for modification as a gunnery target. The basic P-63 was covered with more than a ton of armor, Plexiglas was replaced with heavy bullet-resistant glass, and a pinball-style electric "hit indicator" was installed.

With all this equipment, the RP-63 still was able to do 300 mph at 25,000 feet—swift enough to make it an elusive target for pilots and gunnery crewmen training for combat. The AAF Training Command developed 30-caliber frangible bullets—a combination of lead and plastic that splattered into dust on impact—for firing at the RP-63. The shock of these bullets hitting the armor was recorded on a counting device inside the airplane. A light indicating each hit flashed in the RP-63's cockpit and in its propeller spinner. The program quickly obtained the nickname "pin ball." Thirty-two of these aircraft were built in 1944 and 302, in 1945.

The RP-63 program lacked the glamor of combat aircraft, but it had a new technology slant, and Larry Bell was looking for anything in 1945 that seemed to hold promise for the future.

10

The First

Jet Airplane

The Cleveland Indians night game was a cliffhanger, but Larry wasn't listening. He had fallen asleep in his armchair after dinner, and the voices on the radio spoke only to themselves. Suddenly, Lucille walked in, hesitated for a moment when she saw Larry was asleep, then gently touched his shoulder. "I wouldn't bother you, but it's Washington on the line."

Larry followed her out of the room, wiping his eyes. He listened to someone in the Pentagon asking if he and his chief engineer could come to Washington on the first possible train.

"What's up?"

"General Echols and General Arnold want to see you."

"We'll be there first thing."

He called chief engineer Harlan M. Poyer at home. They boarded a train at midnight, and a cab left them in front of the Pentagon at ten the next morning. As they walked in, Bell brushed off a bit of confetti from Poyer's coat.

"Family party," said Poyer with a smile. "I'm sure they got along fine without me."

Brigadier General Oliver P. Echols, chief of the Materiel Division, described what the air corps knew of the history of gas turbine development in England. The British were already flying jet-propelled aircraft, and through General Arnold's request, British engines were being made available to the United States.

"We've selected General Electric to reproduce about fifteen of these engines," said General Echols. "We're asking your company to build the airplane."

"When do we start?" Bell said, moving forward in his seat.

The general smiled. Bell's instant reaction was something he had expected. Echols had just won a five-dollar bet. "You just did, Larry."

It was September 5, 1941. After lunch, General Arnold held a meeting with Bell, Poyer, and D. R. Shoults of the General Electric Company. The topic was an engine invented by RAF officer Frank J. Whittle in the 1930s and first flown aboard a Gloster E.28/39 on May 15, 1941.

"This engine produces 1,250 pounds of static thrust," said General Arnold. "A two engine fighter should have potent characteristics."

It was agreed that Bell would design and build three airplanes, and General Electric would supply fifteen versions of the British engine design. No one was sure what the Germans and Japanese were up to, so it was important to get the job started fast.

Bell and Poyer sketched ideas on the train back to Buffalo. The next morning, while Bell called together a group of key engineers selected by Poyer, Ray Whitman was on the phone arranging for rental of a former Ford Motor Company plant on Main Street in Buffalo.

"Before I start, will all of you swear an oath of secrecy?" Larry asked.

They did; and Bell told them what he had learned the day before, showing them an 8½ by 11 inch free-hand sketch of the Whittle engine that had been given to him by General Echols. After the meeting, Bell named Edgar P. Rhodes project engineer.

While arrangements were completed for the three-story Main Street facility—in which Ford cars were still being sold by a dealer on the ground floor—the design team worked in the old Pierce-Arrow automobile plant on Elmwood Avenue near Bell's P-39 plant.

When the project moved to the red brick Ford factory, it was guarded twenty-four hours a day and could be entered only with special passes. The car agency moved out overnight. Windows were welded shut, and the lower panes were painted blue. (This color was dominant in all of Bell's plants, because Larry once remarked "nice color" during the dedication of a new building. Employes who were present spread the word. He also liked green and red but spent his working life surrounded by what was known within Bell Aircraft as "Bell blue.")

Cover airplane for the first U.S. jet: The propeller-driven U.S. Navy XP-59, which never got beyond the mockup stage, shown here. The jet was designated XP-59A to imply that it was just a modification of the XP-59.

XP-59A with a dummy propeller attached to its nose to make it look like an ordinary aircraft.

Larry gets a P-59 ride in an observer seat built forward of the cockpit in one of the P-59s.

The FBI went to work screening production workers who might be called into the project. Drinkers, bar-room talkers, and womanizers were ruled out as risks.

Two weeks after the Washington meeting, preliminary design was complete, and Bell got the go-ahead on construction. It would be another five and a half months before the design was completed, but in only three months, on January 9, 1942, work began on assemblies for the new airplane.

To help keep the secret, the airplane was not given an original designation. It was named the XP-59A, implying it was a version of the XP-59 Bell pusher-propeller fighter design that was still in the mock-up stage. (The propeller P-59 project was terminated in late 1941.)

On September 30, 1941, Bell received a fixed-fee contract for $1.6 million to build three XP-59As. Delivery was set for eight months from October 3, and Secretary of War Henry L. Stimson gave personal approval to the project.

Larry Bell often pointed out that while General Electric worked closely with Whittle on the engine, his company "went it alone" on the aircraft. "We received no help [from Gloster]," said Bell. "Frank Whittle provided the kind of temperatures we could expect from the engine and told us how we might protect the fuselage from the jet engine blast and information like that." Lieutenant Colonel Benjamin W. Chidlaw of the Materiel Division was named to head the development and testing phases of the XP-59A.

The extreme secrecy of the jet program was not just wartime security. The British were not unaware of the postwar value of Whittle's development and had insisted that Secretary Stimson agree to several stipulations, including:

—No release of information to a third party without British consent.
—Commercial (postwar) rights would be protected.
—No one but British or U.S. citizens would be permitted to have access to the Whittle information without British consent.

Stimson agreed, and his staff stressed to the air corps, Bell, and General Electric that the U.S. government expected them to live up to this agreement. The result was a Manhattan-Project-style security in Buffalo.

The ground floor of the Main Street facility was made into a machine shop. The aircraft was assembled on the second floor. Some parts had to be made at the Niagara Falls plant, so they were given false labels. The engine exhaust pipe, for example, was marked "heater duct."

About this time, people began to disappear at the Elmwood and Wheatfield plants. A lathe operator or draftsman would come to work in the morning and find that the man next to him suddenly had been replaced by somebody new.

"Hey!" one machine operator exclaimed. "What happened to Harry?"

"I got told this morning to come over here," was the reply. "Who's Harry?"

Men excused themselves from car pools with a standard reply that sounded almost too casual: "Just assigned to a temporary job. No sweat. Be back in the pool in a couple of months." One car pool group went to plant security with the suspicion that a recent dropout might have fled with secret papers.

Employes engaged in the XP-59A project could not tell their families what they were working on or where they were working. If a family emergency arose, the spouse could call an unlisted number. The operator at the Main Street facility would take the information, send it by guard to the employee, and the employee then placed a separate call home.

When the first engine arrived under guard by railway express on August 4, 1942, and the second a few days later, security was further heightened. There was a guard within ten feet of the engines twenty-four hours a day until they were fitted to XP-59A No. 1 and preparations for shipment began.

As unobtrusively as possible on September 10, workmen knocked the bricks out of one wall of the second floor and lowered large crates containing the XP-59A's fuselage and wings to railroad cars. The destination was Muroc, California, in the Mojave Desert, the loneliest U.S. testing place the air corps could find. To assure the high-precision bearings in the engines would not be damaged by vibration, an air compressor system kept the turbine blades turning throughout the trip.

It was a little more than a year after General Arnold's meeting with Larry Bell that the first jet airplane made its trip from Buffalo. An army officer and five enlisted men made the trip with the XP-59A, accompanied by three General Electric personnel assigned to keep the turbines turning. The army contingent's assignment was straightforward—guard the XP-59A with your life!

The guards were kept busy. The fuselage was on one flat car and the wings on another. Next to the fuselage crate was the huge compressor, pumping air noisily into the engine turbines. At every stop, railroad men and curious bystanders asked about the big crates. One veteran railroader, who had seen all types of shipments and never been so puzzled before, said to one of the General Electric engineers: "Send me a telegram collect the minute the war is over, and tell me what's in those crates."

On another occasion, when the jet section was hooked in the middle of a fast freight, one of the military policemen intercepted a brakeman moving forward on the tops of the boxcars. Carrying out his orders to the letter, the guard would not let the brakeman walk through the XP-59A cars. The train had to be stopped so the brakeman could walk around the cars and continue his trip forward.

Chief test pilot Bob Stanley had preceded the shipment west a month earlier and found a mess awaiting the pioneering aircraft in California. He told the contractor hired by the government to build the new base on the north end of Rogers Dry Lake: "We've got something important to do here, and you haven't got a damn thing ready for us."

Stanley went to Los Angeles and found a huge tent that had been used in the past for religious revival meetings. He rented it, just in case it was needed.

What worried Stanley was the knowledge that the civilians had to get out before the airplane arrived. Stanley was known for relentless determination, which he focused on the construction crew. By the time the airplane arrived, the barracks were finished, and the hangar was complete, except for the floor and some electrical wiring. It was September 20, and the air corps/contractor team was notified that the official date for the first XP-59A flight had been set for October 2, less than two weeks away. Assembly of the aircraft began that night.

Under Ed Rhodes's supervision, the craft was ready within a week. On September 26, the engines were scheduled to be run for the first time installed in the airplane. The plane was wheeled out on the dry lakebed and positioned facing the wind.

The left engine was turned over but would not ignite. Then the crew discovered that an excited mechanic had forgotten to remove one of the wooden shipping plugs from an engine air inlet. With the oversight remedied, the engine was tried again. It worked. So did the other engine. Both ran successfully through three five-minute run-ups.

Larry Bell was present on September 30, when Bob Stanley conducted three taxi tests. Stanley was confident of the machine, so he made what he called "some high taxis," lifting the aircraft a foot or two off the lake bed. The actual first flight of the first American jet aircraft was September 30, 1942. Bell stopped Stanley from making further attempts at higher altitudes that evening, although Stanley wanted to fuel up and continue the tests.

The next day, October 1, Stanley brought the aircraft to higher altitudes. Ed Rhodes kept a log of these tests: "Four flights just off the ground were made, wheels down. Nose wheel shimmied some. Adjusted. Then OK. Takeoff distance about 2,000 feet, 80–90 mph, varying heights, 25 to 100 feet. Critical temperatures OK. Fuel cross flow OK." At this time the aircraft carried no serial number or identifying markings other than the U.S. blue disk with a white star. The P-59 was designed to carry two 37-mm cannons and three .50 caliber machine guns, but aircraft number 1 was never fitted with any armament.

There was a large group of government and military brass present for the official first flight, October 2. Bob Stanley's comments were: "Duration of flight: thirty minutes. Throttle was applied promptly and acceleration during takeoff appeared quite satisfactory. . . . The first flight reached an altitude of approximately twenty-five feet."

A total of four flights was made that day. The third was flown by Colonel Lawrence G. Craigie, making him the first U.S. military jet pilot. On the fourth flight, Stanley planned to head for high altitude, but his landing gear vibrated on takeoff and only retracted half way up. He put the gear back down and landed. That was the end of flying for plane No. 1 until October 30.

"You got to 10,000 feet," said Bell, shaking Stanley's hand. "That makes it a respectable day, all around. We've got an airplane, and you proved it."

In the next four weeks, a pair of new engines was shipped in by General Electric's West Lynn, Massachusetts, facility, the landing gear was repaired, and an observer cockpit was installed just in front of the regular cockpit.

At 11:20 A.M. on October 30, the honor of being first U.S. jet

aircraft passenger went to Ed Rhodes, project engineer. Stanley
noted after his first flights with the airplane: "I had less trouble
and fewer mechanical interruptions than with any other prototype I'd ever flown."

As flights continued, the Bell crew was engrossed in an effort
to find the cause for test pilots' complaints of a need for exces-
sive force to move the rudder. Stanley grew increasingly im-
patient. Flying aircraft No. 2 late one afternoon, he landed and
taxied fast, directly at the open hangar. He turned the aircraft
and stopped abruptly, then boosted the jet engines briefly,
blowing exhaust and dust on the Bell men working inside.

Stanley got out of the cockpit and climbed up on the XP-
59A's elevator. "Jack Russell," he shouted to the crew chief.
"Bring a hacksaw out here."

Without hesitation, Russell brought the saw. Stanley cut a
few inches off the top of the rudder, squaring off the rounded
edge. He threw the excess pieces of rudder and the saw to the
ground, walked back to the cockpit and taxied away for takeoff.

"Works much better that way," Stanley said later.

The XP-59A had some similarity to the P-39. The wing was
mounted in the middle of the fuselage to leave room for the two
jet pods slung on each side. Tricycle landing gear let the airplane sit level and gave the pilot good ground visibility. The tail
section was curved upward to keep those surfaces free of the
heat of the jet gasses. The first P-59s had cloth-covered flaps—
but the use of fabric in flying machines was to end upon the
arrival of jet propulsion.

Testing continued, and the engineers realized the engines
which had been copied from the British W2B engine would
never reach the expected level of thrust. In addition, the British
requirement for extreme secrecy barred adequate tests of the
XP-59A's engine intake duct design. The company was refused
permission to use any other than military wind tunnels. The
best of these was at Wright Field. It was inadequate.

In an Institute of the Aeronautical Sciences paper presented
in August 1945, General Electric's Shoults and Col. Donald J.
Keirn reported: "Performance predictions for this aircraft (XP-
59A) were based on estimating design performance characteristics furnished from England in lieu of United States engine
test data. Unfortunately, neither the original nor the later production engines produced the output predicted."

As a result of this and of other requirements for secrecy that prevented interchange with outside technical experts, such as those in NACA and the equipment vendors, the first U.S. jet never reached the performance levels being attained by the best of the contemporary propeller-driven aircraft in the United States and Europe.

The P-59 was to serve as a flying test platform for development of adequate jet engines to power future high performance aircraft. The government's summary of the program on June 28, 1945, said: "Even though a combat airplane did not result from the development of the X and the YP-59A airplanes, it is considered that the development was very worthwhile, since it proved that the principle of jet propulsion for aircraft was sound and practical, and the airplanes themselves will be good training airplanes for pilots who will fly later jet propelled airplanes into combat."

Much of the P-59 effort centered on the engines, which burned kerosene. In the early days, they often produced such dark trails of smoke that the sight alarmed anyone who saw them from the ground or air. Once, a pilot from a Muroc airbase notified his field that a plane had apparently just landed trailing smoke and flames at the XP-59A base. Firetrucks roared up to the gates but were denied entrance or even a reason why they could not enter.

Bad weather hampered the Muroc test program in January and February of 1943. The aircraft had to be moved after heavy rain, because the dry lake bed had filled with water. A new test site thirty-five miles away, was selected, and on March 10, craft No. 2 was wrapped in canvas. A crude, droopy-looking dummy four-bladed propeller was stuck on its nose. Aircraft No. 1 stayed at the Muroc hangar, where work continued on various modifications and revisions needed at the time. But No. 2 got the V.I.P. ride of its life. The highway to Hawes field was shut down for its lone traveler, the XP-59A, whose forty-nine-foot wingspan covered both lanes.

As the special secret airplane, wrapped like a mummy, passed one group of farmers, some bets were made. Most thought they were watching a robot bomb capable of flying from California to Japan.

The delicate engine needed overhaul after each three hours' running. By April 11, 1943, the first XP-59A had made only thirty flights for a total flying time of fifteen and a half hours. General Electric was learning fast, however; and, as time went

Larry in his barracks room at Muroc, 1942.

Wrapped tightly, disassembled P-59 is loaded aboard a boxcar for shipment west.

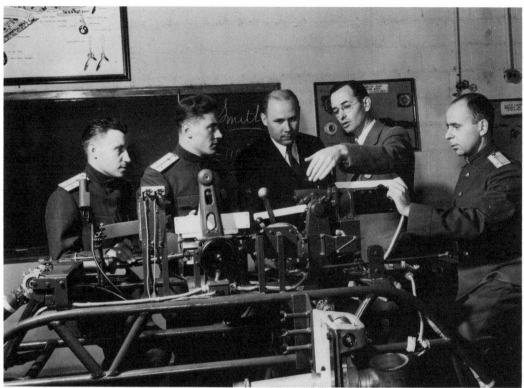

At center is the Soviet Union's World War II representative at Bell Aircraft, Andre Schevshenko, who was shocked in 1944 to learn the P-59 secret. "How could you do this to me," he told Larry. "I'm supposed to know what's going on around here!"

Conference on the field at Muroc. At Bell's right is Bud Kelly.

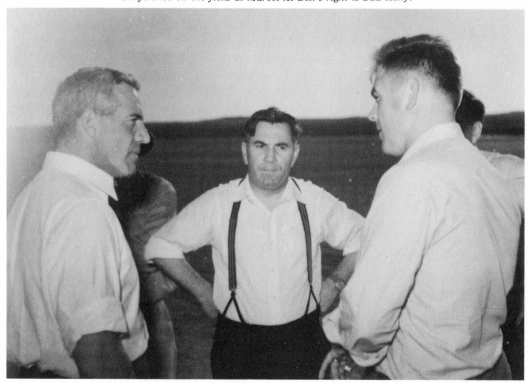

on, it replaced the original 1-A engines with 1-14B units that included several improvements and delivered about 1,400 pounds of thrust.

These early engines were fearsome to behold. They spewed fire like blowtorches. And the Muroc crew was the first to live with the ear-piercing combination whine/roar that in later years was to become as familiar as train whistles were in 1942.

Careless crewmen were also introduced to the power of jet thrust. The Bell flight test log of February 10, 1944, reported: "On this date, Bell inspector E. F. Fisher, weighing two hundred pounds, walked into the jet approximately four feet behind the nozzle while the aircraft was operating at rated power. It lifted him approximately three feet in the air, tumbled him end over end approximately three times, and he made a face-down landing on the concrete surface."

The Bell crewmen had to work long hours, live in barracks, and continue to maintain secrecy, even from nearby air force personnel. Like submariners in the navy, they became close knit and traveled in groups, eventually donning black derby hats as a badge of jet service. In nearby towns, the groups of Bell crewmen were easy to find.

Bell test pilot Jack Woolams combined his hat with some innovations of his own to pull a mammoth practical joke. It happened when some P-38s were flying a training mission in the Muroc area. Suddenly, an aircraft without a propeller showed up from out of the sun. A gorilla in the cockpit wagged his head at the astonished fliers. The interloper wore a black derby hat and puffed a cigar furiously, then dived away and disappeared. The freak event was the subject of countless barroom conversations through the rest of the war.

Larry Bell also had some fun with the P-59 secret before the army made its first announcement of the program on January 6, 1944. He met Guy Vaughn, president of Curtiss-Wright, on a train in 1943.

"Guy," said Bell with a broad smile, "isn't one of your divisions busy making airplane propellers day and night?"

"You know it well, Larry," said Vaughn.

"That's so," replied Bell. "Do you think it will ever be possible to fly an airplane without propellers?"

"Of course not."

"You know, Guy, I have a hunch that someday we'll somehow fly airplanes without propellers."

The two men entered a discussion of whether a propellerless airplane would be as impossible as perpetual motion. "What would keep the airplane moving?" asked Vaughn.

"Let's bet," said Bell. "I bet that within a year we find some way to fly a plane without a propeller. I bet $50."

Vaughn hesitated and looked intently at Bell's grinning face. Then he smiled and without speaking pulled out his wallet. The two men gave the cash to Vaughn's secretary, who promised to pay the winner a year from that date.

It was on this train trip from California that Bell realized he was developing an unreasonable fear. Harlan Poyer and Larry were making their way through the train toward the dining car when Poyer noticed that Bell hesitated at the swaying, clattering connections between cars, and shut his eyes when he walked through.

Bell was pale when they reached the dining car. "Damn it," he told Poyer. "I think I'm getting motion sick." He wiped cold sweat off his brow. They ordered drinks, but Bell didn't eat that night. Larry had developed a phobia almost as strong as his fear of flying, and it stayed with him for the rest of his life.

Larry also disliked riding at the end of the train in his private railroad car based at the New York Central terminal in Buffalo. Signal tower operator Bradley Hilbert recalled that Bell insisted his car never be put on the rear of a train, but at least two or three cars up from the end. "I think he made a special deal with somebody," said Hilbert. "We didn't shuttle cars around like that for anybody else, not even railroad brass."

Bell proposed in June 1943 that the army buy three hundred production model P-59s in addition to the three original experimental models and thirteen YP-59s (advanced models) that were in production. This size order would have absorbed General Electric's entire output of its latest version I-16 engines, leaving none for the navy's new FR-1 jets. And it would have meant that six hundred Bell P-63s would not be produced for the war effort because of the employes diverted to the jet program. The Army Air Force ordered one hundred P-59s on March 11, 1944. Unit cost was estimated at $123,477.

Bell was shocked on October 10, 1944, when he was verbally notified that the entire order was to be terminated with the thirty-ninth airplane. "Hell," said Larry, "why didn't you check with me to find out the most economical way to stop this project. Let's talk it over." The result was a compromise. Bell

First production P-59A-1. Wingtips and rudder are squared—a result of Bob Stanley's on-the-spot modification at Muroc, when he cut the rounded top off an XP-59 rudder with a hacksaw.

One of the reasons the P-59 was too slow for combat was that it had bigger wings than it needed.

would stop work after building fifty of the original one hundred production P-59s ordered. Twenty of these were designated P-59A-1s, and thirty were P-59B-1s.

Records were set by these aircraft. Jack Woolams achieved an unofficial altitude record of 45,765 feet on July 14, 1943, with the original XP-59A. Five months later, he reached 47,600 feet. Some P-59s were used for radio-control tests, completely guided by signals from the ground or from a separate P-59 equipped for airborne radio control.

Most of the aircraft stayed in the army, but five were assigned to the navy, and one was shipped to the British. The best speed ever reached by the P-59 was 425 mph. The airplanes remained in active service until November 30, 1949. That is the last date one of the P-59Bs is mentioned on navy records.

11

Bell's
Georgia Bombers

Telegrams suddenly began arriving from Georgia. Larry received five wires in one day from prominent Georgians, including the governor. Everyone wanted him to make the Jackson Day speech in Atlanta, even though there had been no public announcement of plans for an air force bomber plant.

"This is pretty well organized," Bell told a banker friend born in Georgia. "What do you think of it?"

"Larry, it's Southern politics. They're putting on the charm, and it'll get intense if you accept that speaking engagement. They're a bunch of politicians looking for some business advantage," advised the friend.

"Don't they know there's a war on?"

"That makes no difference."

"By God," said Bell, "I'm going to make that Jackson Day speech, and I'm going to tell them some facts of life. They think they want the big bomber plant, but when they get through, they'll find out we'll take away all their maids and chauffeurs. They'll wish to hell they'd never seen me."

By the time Jackson Day arrived on March 15, the air corps had made its announcement that the plant would be built at Marietta, just north of Atlanta. Ground breaking was scheduled for March 30. Larry Bell was the only one in the room who knew the size of the project that would completely remake the community. He had never had such an attentive audience.

The dinner had been preceded by a cocktail party in the hotel ballroom. Larry had been having trouble with his ulcers

133

and was on the wagon. He declined someone's offer to get him a drink, and after a few minutes he realized no one in the room was drinking. Everyone was standing far away from a long bar at the end of the room, and no one was ordering anything. The bartenders stood alert and exchanged glances of disbelief.

"Say, let me have a scotch and soda, would you please?" said Bell. Mayor Blair smiled as someone handed Bell his drink, and a roomful of people moved to the bar.

Bell selected former U.S. Navy Captain Harry E. Collins as vice president in charge to open the Georgia division. Collins had joined the company in 1940 and had spent much of his life in the South. He set up a temporary office in the Rhodes-Haverty building in Atlanta in May and began the job of supervising the construction of a plant that would contain more than twenty-five thousand workers and produce forty B-29s a month.

The main production building would measure 1,000 by 2,000 feet, stand four and a half stories high, and would require moving nine million yards of dirt. There were several additional buildings and an office building that was separate from the main structure. Larry described the project in a taped interview years later:

"We laid it out. We agreed to be the supervising contractor. We wouldn't build it; it was to be built by some construction-ists, but we were the sponsor for it. We had to sign; we had to be responsible for it and all that sort of thing. For the engineering that we had to do and all the work supervising and so forth and so on, watching the whole damn thing all the way through, do you know what we got for that? What our fee was? For all this responsibility, to make this thing a workable plant, applying our knowledge and so forth and so on? For that we got a fee, to build the whole plant, one dollar!"

With the war underway and blackouts frequent, the plant was built without windows and was completely air conditioned. Photographers had to coax employees to step outside into the summer heat if a picture was needed.

Moving-in day for the first hundred employees took place on March 15, 1943. In the community and in the Georgia Division's *Bell News,* the product everybody was working on was referred to simply as the "Bell Bomber." Because of tight wartime security, no mention of B-29 was made and no picture of the airplane was published until June 17, 1944. By that time, the aircraft were being seen over Japan.

A series of unfortunate incidents involving the plant manager's office brought Bell to the conclusion that while Harry Collins had been ideal as the man to get things started in Georgia, he didn't know enough about production to run the plant. So he moved Collins to the Washington, D.C., office and put Omer L. Woodson in charge of the Georgia Division. In August 1944, Woodson resigned "to accept an executive post as a vice president of the Hughes Tool Company . . . working closely with the well-known aviation figure, Howard Hughes." The resignation had been sudden, and Bell personally took over, temporarily, because there hadn't been time to find a replacement.

"The night Woodson quit," Bell said later, "a cocktail party was held for him. I was called out of the room by a phone call from Howard Hughes, who let me know there was no job at Hughes for Woodson. The man had done a first-class job, but apparently it was too much for him. He had just quit and invented the Hughes job."

Larry discovered that Carl Cover, a former executive vice president of the Douglas Aircraft Company, was in army service but not overseas. He made arrangements to have Cover put on loan as manager of the division. The following December, Cover and Max Stupar, the former supervisor from Buffalo who had been working in Georgia as director of Industrial Planning for the corporate staff, were killed in an airplane crash at Wright Field. A young Georgia attorney, James V. Carmichael, was named to head the plant. He finished out the war and brought the plant to a production level half again as high as the original design. By the end of the war, the plant was producing at a rate of sixty airplanes a month.

Although the first employes had started in March 1943, actual production of the first bomber didn't begin until October. There was some confusion, and to an outsider, the possibilities didn't look promising. A visiting general from Wright Field told Larry, "If you get a machine out by the end of the year, I'll eat it without salt and pepper."

It was a wisecrack, but Bell took it seriously. Once again, there was a deadline to meet, and the plant delivered its first two B-29s before the last day of 1943.

A New Englander, Lieutenant Colonel William A. Altenburg, served as assistant air force resident representative at the Georgia plant. Altenburg was extremely proud of being a Yankee, and the Georgians reacted by directing endless joking remarks at him.

"The Southerners never get over needling a Yankee, some of them," recalled Bell. "It was good-natured, but his life was miserable." Lieutenant Colonel and Mrs. Altenburg had a son whom they named Sherman. A few weeks after the birth of the baby, they invited their Southern acquaintances to a party to celebrate the event. Larry Bell attended the party. "So the party came," he recalled later, "and we all went out there in a group, about thirty of us, men and their wives, to call on the Altenburgs and pay our respects to the baby. There was a sign over the open door at the house that said 'walk in,' so we entered.

"Colonel and Mrs. Altenburg were nowhere to be seen, but in the middle of the living room was baby Sherman in his crib. And along side of him on a stand was a box of kitchen matches. It was Altenburg's way of saying Sherman will burn you down again!"

No one kidded Larry Bell, the man who had brought so many jobs to Marietta. He never forgot an introduction by a prominent Georgian, who greatly pleased Bell by saying, "I'm a Southerner and a good one, but I want to tell you here tonight that you ought to forget Sherman. No matter what you think of him, you ought to forget him. The war's over. We all know what Sherman did, burning down a lot of houses around here, but nowadays let's keep in mind that Larry Bell has spent more money in Georgia, by God, ten to one, than Sherman ever burned up."

After a visit to Georgia, publisher William B. Ziff termed the Bell bomber plant "the South's industrial miracle of the generation." He described it as follows: "How large is this plant? Well, imagine, if you can, nearly two Empire State Buildings laid end to end inside the main building. Under its roof there would be room for twenty of the world's largest battleships with enough vacant space for sixty-nine submarines and twenty-four PT boats."

The industrial miracle at Marietta drew attention from all parts of the nation. Other industrialists were impressed that Bell had been so successful in a rural Southern area. In 1941,

Wartime visitors at the Bell bomber plant in Georgia: From left, O.L. "Woody" Woodson, general manager; Lt. Col. James H. Doolittle; N. Leake of the Bemus Bag Co.; and Larry Bell.

Lt. Col. Altenburg, the New Englander working in Georgia who named his son Sherman.

Marietta had had a total population of eight thousand, and most of the mechanically inclined men had already been drawn to good paying jobs in Atlanta and elsewhere. It was a rural, quiet community. But, under the leadership of Mayor Blair, Marietta carefully planned new subdivisions, recreation centers, and playgrounds. The city limits were expanded 50 percent, so tightly enforced zoning laws would block any hodge-podge development.

After twenty-two thousand production workers had been added to the original eight thousand residents, the *Cobb County Times* reported: "Today Marietta is growing, but without growing pains . . . thanks to careful advance planning. The growth has been orderly, has entailed no impossible burden on the taxpayers, and it is safe to assume that the growth we have experienced will be permanent. There is some regret that quiet, easy-going days are left behind, but there is more of pride . . . in accomplishments and future expectations that Marietta will become the 'Airways of the Southeast.'"

Larry Bell became convinced after the war, as he saw the South continue to develop and draw industry from the North, that the bomber plant had started it all. "I believe," Bell once said, "and other people agree with me, that the B-29 in Georgia was probably the biggest and most successful single manufacturing enterprise in the country during the war. . . . My friends down there have repeatedly told me that the operation of Bell Aircraft probably had more influence on the rebirth of the South than anything that's ever been done."

The Georgia enterprise was also very profitable for Bell Aircraft because of a snap decision made by Larry at a meeting at Wright Field. All the B-29 contractors had been called to a meeting to discuss the army's proposal that they switch from standard cost-plus-fixed-fee (CPFF) contracts to a flat price per aircraft. The idea was not popular. There were no volunteers, so the general conducting the meeting finally called for a show of hands. Larry's hand was the only one that went up. Boeing, North American, and General Motors stuck with cost plus.

"So we changed to flat price," Bell recalled, "and thank God we did, because all they made on CPFF was about 2 percent, and we averaged about 9.9. Most of the money Bell Aircraft made [during World War II] was in Georgia, just because we took the gamble of flat price, which was exactly what the government wanted."

It was a native son of Marietta who told the first Bell B-29 combat story for his home town. Major Jack R. Millar, Jr. requested a Marietta-built airplane and got it, and he reported that it behaved "as beautifully as junior does on Sunday after services when the minister drops by for fried chicken and buttermilk." He reported that the air force's first B-29 raid from China to Yawata was the longest ever flown in aviation warfare; then: "Finally, the great moment came for the 'Georgia Peach' to drop her 'seeds.' We were on our bomb run. The big bomb bay doors opened . . . the bombardier hovered over his bombsight . . . the navigator had just given me a heading . . . the copilot and the gunners scanned the skies, keeping a sharp lookout for enemy fighters . . . the engineer watched over his instruments carefully, assuring me that everything was perfect . . . the radio operator sat tensely beside his set waiting for the 'bombs away' signal to tap out his message to our home base that we had dropped our 'seeds' and were heading for home.

"Then . . . 'bombs away!' We were all thrilled, scared, and excited to know that we had actually dropped death and destruction in the first raid on the Japan homeland by land-based aircraft. We saw great fires on the ground and knew that our bombs had done considerable damage. The Jap broadcast said we bombed the residential section, the hospital, and the schools . . . well, all I can say is that they must have these institutions in their factories. It's not the policy of the Army Air Force to bomb these places—and we didn't.

"We hit at the heart, and the heart is the factories. If we can knock them out, we will have thrown a big wrench in the Nip war effort."

Major Millar, who had done some writing for the *Cobb County Times* in his high school days, returned to the United States with the Georgia Peach late in the war to Colorado Springs, Colorado, to train B-29 combat crews.

The plant had a severe crisis in its early days. Just as the production program had gotten started, a quality inspector made public charges that Bell's bombers were being improperly manufactured and were unsafe and sent letters to congressmen and senators. Bell responded by calling in the FBI and army intelligence. At a meeting that resulted, Bell asked the inspector, "By the way, let me see your pilot's license again, will you?"

The inspector opened his wallet, mentioning his days as a paratrooper and pilot, and handed Bell a document.

"This is remarkable," said Bell. "Have you shown it to the other fellows?" The man said no, so Bell handed it to an FBI agent, who silently passed it to the rest of the men in the room. It was a Georgia fishing license.

But the wheels had been set in motion and could not be stopped. It was determined that a board of investigation must be conducted to satisfy the forces in Congress. A colonel that Bell considered "cruel, pretty darned mean, disagreeable, and dangerous, from my standpoint," was put in charge of the investigation. At a meeting with the colonel, Bell explained that the plant had made only ten aircraft and that the quality of the first ten was never as good as it would be with the first ten of the second batch of one hundred. There was some discussion, and finally Bell said, "Well, let's go out and look at the machines."

Later, Larry recalled: "Of course, I had been out there [on the production floor] before, and I knew what I was talking about. But he didn't. We went out, he and I, and we looked over the machines."

Pointing out some scratches and minor dents, Bell said: "This is a little messy. But they're strong and safe. There are a few little scratches and a few little things around there that destroy what looks like a good piece of merchandise, but they're sound enough."

The two men walked from aircraft to aircraft, with Bell doing most of the talking.

"I knew what I was doing," recalled Bell. "I came up along side another one and said—this you can't fault, either. But then we came up to another one, and I said, 'Gee, this is funny. I guess I'm wrong. This is a dog. Look at those wrinkles. Look at those bad rivets.'"

The colonel began taking notes, and Larry went around the aircraft pointing out its faults.

"I was ruthless pointing out the defects. It was terrible. We got inside, and we crawled to look, and I showed everything that was lousy, and then we went up in the cockpit and I showed him what was wrong up there."

The colonel was sitting in the pilot's seat when Bell exclaimed in a tone that sounded surprised: "Do you see that?"

"What do you mean?"

"The nameplate! Boeing Number 12!"

The Boeing aircraft had been flown in for modifications. Bell survived the investigation and went on to build 663 B-29s before the end of the war. All were tested and flown away from the plant without a single accident. Total sales for the division were $230 million, but at the end of the war the plant was shut down swiftly and with a great deal of waste.

Bell had postwar plans for the Niagara Frontier Division, and there was some hope for future work at the Ordnance Division. But in Georgia, as the end of the war neared, management prepared five thousand telegrams to stop work by subcontractors.

"We just dropped the curtain, that's all," said Bell. "It was all over. I remember distinctly, how much money we put in tools and things of that sort. . . . But when we started to liquidate, we cut up finished airplanes that weren't yet ready to fly, took the engines out and things like that, and cut them up with welding torches in the hangar, poured about a foot of sand all over the floor, and sold the pieces for five or ten cents a pound including all the tools.

"One Sunday, I saw five gondola cars loaded with tools that we had sweated blood to get, going to be melted up for scrap. It was sad. We worked too quick. For sixty days, I had a camera set up in the factory to take a picture at eleven o'clock every morning to tell us exactly what had happened. You never saw so damned much destruction in your life as there was getting rid of that stuff."

The same disaster struck the work force that had been trained at great expense and had performed so well. Hiring continued right to the end, and a peak of 28,280 employes was reached in 1945. "They were laid off," said Bell. "I think it took us about two days to lay off nearly thirty thousand people. Of course, our books were in good shape, and we worked all night. It was just like putting sausage through."

Larry Bell recalled with bitterness that, for some reason, the government had not given a production award to the Georgia work force. The other divisions won all the awards possible. "We never got one for the Georgia plant," said Bell. "Not one. I don't quite know what it was or why, because if anything ever worked like a dream—you've heard of a walking dream?—well, this was a walking dream."

12

Total Effort
for Defense

At the end of 1941, the best-dressed men in America wore uniforms and carried rifles. Next best was the man who carried a lunch pail to a defense plant. Workers from other industries stood in line to get jobs at Bell. Everybody wanted to be part of the national effort.

Bell Aircraft's product line had grown to include rear gun enclosures, elevators, and stabilizer assemblies for the B-17 Flying Fortress and gun mounts for all types of aircraft. Gun mount production was so busy it soon would be separated as the Bell Ordnance Division.

Larry received an urgent telephone call from Washington the morning after the Pearl Harbor attack. Two hundred fifty gun mounts were needed in California as soon as possible. "They'll be there," said Bell, hanging up the phone and moving toward the shop.

Then he did something he had done repeatedly when pressure was on. Bell went out on the production line to personally tell each man how important it was to get the work done. "They're counting on us," he'd say. "Let's show them we've got what it takes."

Two hundred fifty gun mounts was a month's production; Bell had them done in two days. At midnight, December 10, the final seventy mounts were flown out of the Buffalo airport on an American Airlines plane.

Three days later, the company went on a seven-day schedule, and just before Christmas, the first group of twenty women production workers started at the Elmwood plant. The company was clattering with activity on December 14, when Larry Bell received a telephone call from General Arnold. The general gave Bell his choice of building a B-29 bomber plant in one of three areas where sufficient labor pools existed: Atlanta, Chicago, or Milwaukee.

"I'll take Georgia," said Bell. "I've had enough of the North Pole."

Opening new territory for aircraft production was nothing new to Bell, who had supervised the building of Martin's plant in Cleveland and had helped Major Fleet relocate in California. He scheduled a trip to Georgia to meet community leaders, but on his way to the airport, Larry checked in at the little country shop of Arthur M. Young, an engineer he had contracted a month earlier to develop helicopter concepts.

When Young had met Bell at a hotel in Washington and described his flying scale model, Larry had one question: "Can it auto-rotate?" Young assured him that the model could, in fact, descend gently if its engine quit. "Bring it to Buffalo, and I'll take a look at it," said Bell.

On May 1, 1942, Young was set up in a small building at Union and Lesser Roads, Gardenville, south of Buffalo, and went to work on a full-scale machine. He and a crew of six engineers and draftsmen worked in isolation from the war effort. Thus, in the early months of 1942, Larry Bell had decided to enter a new business. It was an amazing decision, considering the fact that Bell:

—Was building the first U.S. jet airplane, the XP-59A.
—Was preparing for the ground breaking of a huge Bell bomber plant in Marietta, Georgia.
—Made plans to establish a separate Ordnance Division.
—Was preparing to open a modification center capable of equipping a full range of military aircraft for various special missions.
—Opened Camp Cataract to train the soldiers who would maintain the P-39s.
—Started another addition at the Niagara Falls plant, this time an $8.5 million factory and office space facility.

All this was in addition to his regular duties as manager/chief salesman of a company that was hiring hundreds of men and women weekly to boost fighter aircraft production to nearly six times his five-a-day promise to William Knudsen. Bell seemed to be involved personally in everything. He worked a seven day week, sometimes sixteen and twenty hours a day. Larry was in his office late one second shift when something unusual brought him to the window. A pickup truck was driving across the plant lawn to the main lobby. "What the hell's this?" he said, walking down the hall.

When he got to the lobby Larry was stunned. There in the middle of the floor, Nurse George was working on a badly injured pilot who had been brought in by one of the farmers north of the plant. "Tell me what to do, and I'll help," Larry told the nurse. They put clips on a gash that had penetrated the man's skull and applied a pressure bandage. The swift operation stopped the bleeding and saved a young army pilot's life.

Later, it was learned the rescue squad had raced across the airport to a P-39 crash scene not knowing that a farmer was already bringing in the pilot. Miss George had been the only one left behind at the first aid station. The pilot returned to thank both of them a few months later. "She told me I made a good assistant," said Bell proudly as he shook the man's hand.

Lucille saw very little of Larry, but was with him at all official ceremonies requiring her presence throughout the war. She was at his side when President Roosevelt and Eleanor Roosevelt made separate visits to the Bell facilities, as well as on other occasions when important visitors made it appropriate for Larry to have his wife with him.

Overseas, aircraft built for the French and British but reconverted were put into action for the first time by the U.S. Army, and stories of success sent back through official channels were printed in the plant publications.

Second Lieutenant Richard D. Kent reported in *Bell Ringer*: "The four of us continued our fight for a while when we became engaged in a dog-fight with about twelve Japs. Suddenly, a Zero started to pull up over me. I fired, all the P-39's guns working, and saw the tracers cover him from nose to tail. He blew up directly over me, with a few burning parts falling in front of me. I banked my P-39 in time to see him crash into the water."

One pilot noted that "a captured Jap officer, upon being questioned, answered in perfect English that the 'long-nosed bombers' had greatly demoralized their troops."

There was, however, the phrase "despite what some have

claimed" in one report. The heavy, slow-climbing Airacobra was no match for the Zero. But to Bell employees, the P-39 seemed to be winning the war. Sales manager Fred Schoellkopf, who held an army reserve commission, wanted to get into the fight, flying P-39s, and quietly made arrangements to join a combat squadron. Schoellkopf called Bell in Washington. "Larry, I've decided to enter the Army Air Corps as a fighter pilot."

"Why not wait until I get back into Buffalo, and we'll talk this over?"

"I expected you to say that, Larry," replied Schoellkopf. "I'm already in."

Schoellkopf never flew P-39s in combat, but by the time he returned home in late 1943 to recover from malaria, he had won the Distinguished Flying Cross and Air Medal and had flown more than seventy combat missions in Europe and North Africa.

On the home front, P-39 test pilots worked day and night to get aircraft accepted for army service. It was dangerous work, but monotonous. Several pilots livened things by flying under the Peace Bridge between Buffalo and Canada or under one of the three bridges over the Niagara gorge. This angered the bridge authorities, who fought back by issuing cameras to take pictures of any offending aircraft. Finally they got what they wanted. Larry received the following complaint from the Niagara Falls Bridge Commission:

"On Sunday, July 19, 1942, at 3:55 P.M. and again at 4:45 P.M. a new plane, identified as one of your manufacture, flew under the Rainbow Bridge. This has also occurred on other occasions, and as recently as two weeks ago a plane of your manufacture flew under Rainbow Bridge, New York Central Bridge, and Whirlpool Rapids Bridge.

"Assuming that these planes may be from either your Buffalo or Niagara Falls, N.Y., plants and confident that this practice would not be condoned by yourself or those in authority at either plants, I deemed it advisable to communicate with you a view to preventing a repetition of such action. With the power houses located below the bank within this area, and the danger of causing damage to the Bridges, as well as the possibility of cracking up the plane, it would appear that a word of warning to the boys would suffice."

Bell checked into the matter and sent the following reply:

"With respect to the incidents mentioned in your letter of July 21, involving the flight of a P-39 airplane under the Niagara Falls Rainbow Bridge, as well as the New York Central and Whirlpool Rapids bridges, I wish to state that the party responsible for the incidents has been removed from the employ of this organization, and I do not feel that a recurrence of this circumstance should happen again. I thank you for calling this undesirable condition to my attention."

Actually, Bell could not fire the pilot involved—Second Lieutenant Walter MacMurray—because Bell wasn't his employer. The young army pilot was temporarily grounded, instead, by his superior, a colonel in charge of army test pilots at Bell.

"The colonel pointed out to me the odds against safely flying between the stone walls of the gorge under all three bridges," MacMurray said later. "I was impressed. It was clear I shouldn't have been able to make it!"

In 1942, the Russians reported "The Airacobra is ideal for conditions here, as it cannot ground-loop nor turn over on its nose—two normal bugbears" for regular aircraft. They said the "nosewheel helps in landings, as altitude is hard to judge over snow."

There were jobs at Bell for everyone. Burgard High School conducted a training program for two hundred WPA workers to give them the skills needed for the aircraft production line. Tough, determined men like Max Stupar, production chief at the Elmwood plant, made sure that line kept going: "We're like bowlers, who, instead of rolling the ball down the alley ourselves, let somebody else do it, and then stand in the gutters ready to kick it out."

The pace never slackened. One day after a meeting in Bell's office, public relations director Stephen E. Fitzgerald told his secretary, Elsa Spitznagel: "Larry's the only man I know who should take a sleeping pill in the morning just so other people can keep up with him."

The influence of Larry Bell and his company grew tremendously. In a nearby community, a group of veterans formed Grover E. Bell VFW Post 959 in memory of Bell's brother. The Jewish War Veterans gathered $50,000 to buy a P-39, which they presented to Bell on July 10, 1942, the seventh anniversary of the company. Rabbi Joseph L. Fink asked protection from the "Father of the Universe upon the young men who soon will fly this Airacobra against the mortal enemies of all free men."

When shipping became a problem, a special fuel tank was developed so fighters could be ferried over the same air routes being used by long-range bombers. A 350 gallon tank between the main wheels greatly increased the P-39's range.

The first test airplane with this installation was christened the "Queen Mary," a heavy lady that hauled a total of 460 gallons. The effectiveness of the installation was proved by chief test pilot Jack Woolams, who made a nonstop flight from March Field, California, to Bolling Field, Washington, D. C., on October 2, 1942. The 2,290 mile flight is believed to be the first nonstop cross-country flight of an American fighter. When Woolams landed, he still had 94 gallons of fuel in his main tank. The flight showed Bell was ready to start shipping Airacobras to Russia by way of Alaska. By war's end, more than five thousand Bell fighters would be flown from Niagara Falls to Russia.

Throughout most of 1941, Bell engineers worked with air corps representatives from Wright Field on preliminary design of a successor to the heavy and underpowered P-39. They wanted a reasonably light, fast climbing, highly maneuverable fighter.

Initially, they tried installing laminar flow wings on a P-39E, but it didn't make enough difference in performance. The project evolved into development of the P-63 Kingcobra, which had laminar flow wings to increase speed by reducing drag and an engine boosted by an auxiliary, hydraulically coupled supercharger. It was a return to the idea Bob Woods had designed into the original prototype XP-39A. By providing supercharged air to increase engine horsepower and making the airplane capable of performing at higher altitudes, the P-63 was effective 10,000 feet higher than the P-39. It had twice the P-39's range and an extra 125 horsepower.

The first flight of the XP-63A was made by Bob Stanley on December 7, 1942. He later flew the aircraft to 37,000 feet. Stanley compared its performance with the British Spitfire, "which had endeared itself to all pilots who have ever flown it."

Jack Woolams, who was to have many misadventures as a flier before his death following the war, destroyed the first XP-63A in a crash at Muroc, California, in January 1942. He had flown the airplane from Niagara Falls to the desert base for a series of tests, when a universal joint broke and the main landing gear failed to come down all the way.

It was becoming dark by the time he had gone through the manual on wheel-lowering techniques and burned off his remaining fuel. The field lights were supposed to be on at the head of the runway, but by mistake the lights on the side of the strip were turned on. Woolams landed without wheels in a field of small trees. He was unhurt but the aircraft was destroyed.

A month later, the second XP-63 was completed, and the tests continued. The airplane proved to be a first-class fighter, capable of climbing and maneuvering with the best in the world, and Bell tooled up for production. Although the new fighter closely resembled the P-39 in appearance, not one structural part was interchangeable.

When the P-63 entered production in early fall of 1943, the work force at Bell Aircraft's Niagara Frontier Division (Elmwood and Niagara Falls plants), was 59 percent women. Most had never before been inside a factory gate, but through training and strategic shifting of supervisors, the switch to P-63 production was made without stopping the P-39 line.

The Kingcobra was well insulated because most were destined to fly the northern route into Russia. Of 2,971 built by the end of the war, 2,453 went north. The U.S. Army Air Force got 403, and the Free French, 112.

The first leg of the ferry flight was from Niagara Falls to Great Falls, Montana. Then the army flew them more than two thousand miles to Ladd Field at Fairbanks, Alaska, where Russian pilots took over. The Soviet Union's representative in Buffalo was Andre Schevshenko, whose desk was a few feet away from a movie screen in the next room where secret films of the first American jet, the XP-59A, were repeatedly shown. He knew nothing of the P-59 project until it was announced in the newspapers. It was to be the shock of Schevshenko's life. "I'm supposed to know what's going on around here," he told Larry.

When the production line was running twenty-four hours a day and combat-ready aircraft were being flown across the top of the world directly to the hottest current Soviet battlefronts, letters of praise poured out of Russia. Colonel Peter S. Kiselev said the P-39 "held a very definite advantage over the Messerschmitt 109," and that Soviet pilots felt "it could out-man,

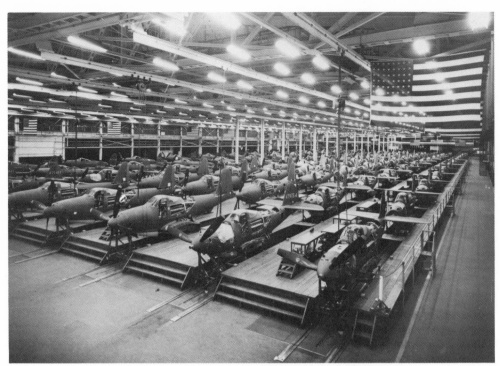

The P-39/P-63 assembly line at Bell's Niagara Falls plant.

Arthur Young at his farm in Pennsylvania flying one of the many scale models he built in perfecting his two-bladed helicopter concepts.

Soviet Kingcobras head north to Alaska over Niagara Falls. Russian pilots flew them from Alaska to the Eastern Front.

The XP-77A in flight.

From the top: XP-77, P-39, P-63, P-59.

out-climb, and out-speed any enemy aircraft," although he qualified the statement by saying that all fighting on the Soviet front is done at roughly three thousand five hundred to ten thousand feet.

Major Vassily Kolibelnikov reported at length on the feats of the "Stalin Falcons" and said the Nazis would not go into battle with the Airacobra "unless they had numerical superiority."

The Russians gave the name "Cobrushka" (little cobra) to the aircraft. Donald Nelson, chairman of the War Production Board, said, "All over Russia, it was the same story. They put the Airacobra, manufactured by the Bell Aircraft Corporation, first [among lend-lease items]; then followed our Jeeps, which they call 'Willys'; and then, our two-and-a-half-ton trucks, which they call 'Studebakers.'"

Toward war's end, the top hero of the USSR Army Air Forces was Lieutenant Colonel of the Guards A. I. Pokryshkin, who shot down fifty-nine Nazi aircraft, forty-eight of them with Airacobras. He was credited as the top Allied ace of World War II. There were ceremonies, and some medals were handed out. President Roosevelt awarded the U.S. Distinguished Flying Cross to Colonel Pokryshkin, and a lieutenant general of the USSR listed ten "heroes of the USSR" who shot down twenty or more enemy planes with Airacobras.

Through most of the war, Bell had pursued a development program for a lightweight fighter that might be a valuable asset if the nation needed a fast interceptor to protect its shores against invaders. The old-time ton-and-a-half fighters had grown to nearly three tons for the Airacobra and four tons or more for some of the bigger escort planes.

"My idea is to go the reverse route," said Bob Woods at a meeting with Bell. "Go back to basic simplicity—building a plane that meets that magic 4-4-4 combination. . . ."

"Four hundred horsepower, 400 miles an hour, no more than 4,000 pounds," Bell agreed.

Preliminary studies started in late 1941. Within a few months, Woods convinced Bell that he could design an airplane able to meet army speed, altitude, and maneuverability requirements. Larry took the concept to Wright Field.

The aircraft was given the designation XP-77 and went under army contract in April 1942. Originally, it was to have a metal fuselage and wings of molded plywood, but metal shortages were being experienced so the engineers went a step further and decided to make the entire airframe of Sitka spruce.

Bell craftsmen were not accustomed to working with wood, so the entire project was subcontracted. Like the P-63, the airplane had a low-drag laminar flow wing. Whenever an improvement was suggested, it was checked to see how much weight it meant. When the finished product was rolled out, the XP-77 was only about fifty pounds overweight at 3,543 pounds.

Bob Woods had reached back into the 1930s' Model 3 file, pulling out some of the best concepts that he had put into the design of the airplane that ran second only to the P-39 in the army's 1937 fighter competition. The XP-77 cockpit was almost an exact duplicate of the cockpit of the Model 3. And, although it was a much smaller airplane, the XP-77 incorporated the Model 3's basic concept: a 12-cylinder engine in front of the pilot, but still back far enough from the propeller to leave room for a tricycle landing gear and a center-line cannon, as well as other armament.

The problems of setting up wooden aircraft production techniques, and getting the job done at a variety of job shops, slowed production of the XP-77. It wasn't until April 1, 1944 that Jack Woolams made the first test flight at Niagara Falls before a crowd of engineers and company executives. It was a success. The XP-77 had attained the 4-4-4 combination (although the Ranger V-12 engine cheated a little, at 520 horsepower). If the United States had needed its own tiny, deadly Spitfire before the end of the war, the XP-77 might have been called upon in great numbers. As it was, the nation neither ran out of aluminum nor needed an interceptor fighter.

When the air force announced the craft's existence on February 8, 1945, it was described as an experimental craft that was helping make important contributions to future warplane development.

Larry sometimes rebelled against the loneliness and pressure of being top man. "Being president is no longer a question of running your business—It's a question of keeping your business from running, and killing, you." He told Dave Forman, "I need a hobby. Go buy me some hunting rifles and shotguns."

"Any particular kind?"

"The kind everybody uses."

The dozen rifles were never fired, at least not by Larry. They ended up as a display in the "Frontier Room," something to look at while drinking coffee before a directors' meeting, like the huge stuffed buffalo head that protrudes from a wall of that room.

Bell once told Forman to buy fishing tackle and equipment—"everything I need for a first class fishing expedition." There was no fishing trip, and the equipment later disappeared, as did Larry's rifles.

The pressures began to show in Larry's face. He became pale, overweight, and increasingly nervous. Late in the day, his eyes seemed out of focus.

General Arnold was having dinner with the Bells in their home at 845 LeBrun Road, in the Buffalo suburb of Eggertsville, when he noticed this condition and felt a twinge of sympathy for the man upon whom he'd laid such burdens.

"Larry," said Arnold, "do you remember the first time we met?" Bell smiled and shrugged. "We met at Rockwell Field, San Diego, in the summer of 1915."

"I remember, now."

"I was out there with some other officers getting checked out in a new Martin plane. You were doing the talking, and you knew your stuff. You made a good impression, Larry."

Bell smiled, and the two men exchanged a silent toast.

13

The Bell
Helicopters

The light at the intersection was slow to change, and war news droned from the radio. A misty rain swirled with the heavy morning traffic. Larry seemed uncomfortable and smoked nervously, while Irene Bernhardt sat quietly in the passenger seat. "Let's see what's going on in Gardenville," he said, abruptly turning into a parking lot and heading back to the intersection.

The helicopter workshop was alive with activity. In the center of the room, nearly complete, was the first full-sized helicopter that Art Young had built in all his years of helicopter research and testing.

"Taking shape nicely," he told Bell. "We'll be ready for engine run-ups by Christmas."

Larry slowly walked around the "Model 30" built by some of Bell's best creative craftsmen who had been pulled off the routine of P-39 production.

"Beautiful scale-up of your little flyer," said Bell.

"Hardly a change."

"There's been slippage in deliveries out here because of war-time priorities," said Bell. "But call me if there are any more problems. I want to see it fly."

Working with Young were about thirty men, including a bright young apprentice named Bartram Kelley. A few months earlier, Larry had assigned Dave Forman to supervise the project. "It needs to be managed," Bell told Forman. "Young gets things done by waving his arms around."

155

On December 24, 1942, the men dragged the craft out the door to a gravel and cinder yard behind the shop. It was a simple one-seat machine powered by a 160-hp Franklin piston engine which turned a single two-bladed rotor and an anti-torque propeller on the tail.

An important feature was auto-rotation. The rotor was free to continue turning if the engine quit, designed to assure a slow, safe descent. Also important in Young's design was a stabilizer bar—a five-foot steel rod weighted at both ends and fastened to the rotor mast just under the blades. This bar acted as a fly-wheel on a hinge. It kept the rotor blades level and independent from the movements of the fuselage. The concept solved the problem of stability that plagued all early helicopters.

Art Young climbed in and started the engine. One of the tubular legs was on a bathroom scale in an effort to measure lift as he gradually increased rotor speed to 150 rpm. The blades made a distinctive whop-whop-whop sound, and the craft strained against the tie-downs. Young stopped the engine and climbed out excitedly. For more than thirteen years since he had left college, he had been ridiculed as a dreamer who built toy-sized helicopters that crashed one after another at his farm in Pennsylvania. The moment he lived for had come.

"I could feel it beginning to lift," he said breathlessly.

Young shut down the test and had the craft dragged back inside. That night, Bart Kelley made this notation: "A.M.Y. would probably have tried to hover if we had not had two public relations visitors."

On the twenty-ninth, Young flew to five feet, while tethered, and test pilot Floyd Carlson hovered to one foot. Although lift-off had been predicted to take place at 260 rpm, it actually occurred at 240 rpm.

In early January, chief test pilot Bob Stanley came out from the main plant. Stanley felt it was time he assessed Model 30, so after studying the craft, he climbed into the seat and flashed thumbs up. It was a cold day, and a gusty wind was blowing. The craft's recently installed directional controls were still on trial. At first, the test went well. Stanley held the craft at about four feet off the ground and gently moved it forward and back, side to side. But suddenly, the helicopter bucked wildly, pop-ping up and down as though it had hiccups. Stanley was tossed out of the seat and up into the rotor blades just as the tail section bucked up into the rotor. The helicopter came down hard with its tail sheared off. Stanley had been caught in the stomach and was thrown outward into a snow pile. He broke a wrist and was shaken. The helicopter was badly damaged.

Stanley was helped into the garage, where he lay on his back on a desk and phoned Larry: "I'm sorry," he said painfully, "but I've delayed your helicopter a little."

The next morning, Larry told Stanley to assign a pilot to the helicopter project. "And get seat belts in that thing," said Bell. Stanley selected Carlson, one of the company's newest experimental test pilots. "I've never seen a helicopter," Carlson had said a few weeks earlier when Stanley sent him to Gardenville. "Go take a look," Stanley had replied.

In later years, Bell recalled that, from Stanley's point of view, Carlson was probably selected because he was the youngest, newest flyer. "But as it turned out," Bell continued, "I think it was one of the most important choices in our history. The helicopter and an able pilot learned to fly together. Floyd probably became the world's best helicopter pilot, certainly the best test pilot, and he soon attained more flying hours than any other helicopter pilot in the world."

By early July, the helicopter team had eliminated the bucking vibration problem and had the machine flying regularly around the field across from the Gardenville shop. Between flights, Carlson worked with the engineers and mechanics, getting to know the machine as well as anyone on the project.

On July 30, the aircraft was trucked to a nearby airport to give it more room for the expanding test program. It was a Friday afternoon, great weather for flying, and the field was busy. Several weekend pilots walked over to see the contraption with a rotary wing. Bart Kelley's notes on the tests that day include this line: "Amid wisecracks of local light airplane pikers, the rotor was started, and Floyd went to town."

Larry witnessed several flights and became convinced that Model 30 was becoming a saleable product. "Art, I'm going to start bringing some government people out here," Bell told Young. "It's time to start promoting this craft."

There had been delays in obtaining materials for the first two aircraft, since experimental helicopters had no wartime priority. But under the contract signed by Bell and Young, November 1, 1941, all of Young's patents were assigned to the company only if the company built two full-sized helicopters within one year. By agreement, the time limit was extended.

Larry went to see General Echols, head of air corps procurement. "I need a priority to build a half-dozen of these helicopters," said Larry. "This project won't interfere with our war production effort, and helicopters are going to be important to the future of aviation."

"I can give you only one kind of priority, Larry," said Echols. "You've got Priority J."

"Never heard of it," said Bell.

"It's the best I can do. What it means is, you can legally build six helicopters. You may not be able to get the materials, but at least you won't go to jail for doing something illegal."

"I'll settle for that."

At the time, Larry's company was spending millions of dollars for materials from suppliers and contractors. It was not difficult for him to obtain the needed supplies, as he put it, "by various types of bootlegging and everything else." He told the head of one supply company, "Certainly, you can find some way to run some extra stuff through for this product important to future national defense?"

Larry invited Dr. Lewis and other officials of NACA to spend two days at Bell and review the garage workshop helicopter program. After the first day, it was apparent from their remarks that they considered Bell's approach crude by NACA standards.

"Larry, you're being hampered by the war effort," said Dr. Lewis. "This project is never going to get any place the way it's being handled."

"You might consider turning it over to NACA," said another visitor. "We could develop it in a proper and cautious manner."

"I don't agree," Bell said bluntly. "You government gentlemen do a great job with your teams of engineers, scientists, mathematicians, and wind tunnels. There are a lot of jobs you're good at."

"What's the point, Larry?" asked Dr. Lewis.

"The point is, if government was as efficient as you imply, *it* would have invented the airplane, not the Wright brothers. Free enterprise did the pioneer work, the building, testing, and demonstrating. NACA was born later, considerably later."

Larry's guests started to speak, but Bell held up his hand. "After we get a little further along and it becomes an industry, sure, NACA can do wonders for us. But not in the beginning."

"The best of luck, Larry," said Dr. Lewis.

The company began an aggressive demonstration and development program. On May 10, 1944, Carlson flew in a Buffalo armory before a massed audience of Civil Air Patrol pilots and cadets. It was the first indoor helicopter flight in the United States.

Then there was the dramatic rescue flight for Jack Woolams, who crashed a plane near Lockport in January 1945, and a rescue of two ice fishermen two miles out on Lake Erie on March 14. The ice on which they had been marooned for twenty-one hours was too soft to hold the helicopter's wheels, so Carlson gently lowered the craft and held it there while the men climbed aboard and were flown to safety, one at a time.

On March 8, 1946, a two-seat improvement on the Model 30, the Bell Model 47, was awarded the world's first commercial certification, NC-1H. There couldn't be any commercial sales without this license, and in 1946, Larry had no interest in developing anything he couldn't sell. The company had applied for the license and the FAA's chief pilot, Raymond Malloy, came to town. He had little previous experience with helicopters, so Carlson had to teach him how to fly the machine before he could do solo evaluation trials.

His only serious complaint was the great amount of physical strength needed to move the control stick. This was alleviated by addition of an irreversible control system, and the license was granted with the stipulation that the model would undergo major overhaul—completely tearing down the machine—after each twenty-five flying hours. "That's not very practical, but it's enough to get us started," said Bell.

The door was open to commercial sales, but since there was no helicopter production line—only a few experimental models—Bell had to assure the board of directors that the time had come to spend some money setting up production. There were several meetings at which Bell stressed one point: "The only way we can sell the helicopter is to have the courage to build some."

At this time, the board included Bell, Whitman, Beard, Woods, Ansley Sawyer, Walter Yates, J. Fred Schoellkopf, Jr., Charles Criqui, and some newcomers—John E. Bierwirth, president of the New York Trust Company, Frederick F. Robinson, president of the National Aviation Company, and John W. deForest, Aetna general agent. "They gave us everything!" Larry exclaimed as he walked into Julius Domonkos' office from the board meeting. "We asked for five hundred helicopters, expecting approval for something less. We got the works."

Bell Model 47s, fresh from the production line, could be purchased in 1946 for $25,000. Dealer discount brought the price to $21,500, and nearly everyone who bought a helicopter listed himself as a dealer.

But things didn't go as Larry planned. His close relationships in the military had faded with the new world that emerged after World War II, and there were few military sales. The machines that left the plant were sold one-by-one, chiefly to commercial operators.

Forman was named manager of the Helicopter Division, a job that involved everything from getting the helicopters built to serving as chief helicopter salesman. He and Larry sold some progressive Chicago leaders on starting a helicopter mail service for that city. A few helicopters were sold to the air force, and then a dozen were sold to Argentina to spray swarms of locusts. There were immediate reports of success and of some disasters.

In Oregon, a young pilot tried joy riding, and his helicopter crashed on a golf course. Forman and crew of specialists got to the scene as fast as possible to check for a mechanical cause for the crash. Not once did the Bell team or the FAA find any cause other than pilot error, but doubts about the safety of helicopters persisted.

The question in the public's mind was expressed by a reporter who interviewed Igor Sikorsky—Bell's chief helicopter competitor—during one of Sikorsky's visits with Larry in Buffalo. "What happens if the rotor comes off?" asked the reporter.

"That is not recommended," Sikorsky replied.

Bell and Sikorsky were friends who closely followed each other's progress. Their attitude was this: No one company alone is going to develop a whole new form of transportation. In Canada, a dozen Bell helicopters were put to work on a huge dam project. "It's a miracle operation," Forman reported after a trip north. "They operate in narrow canyons and little hilltops where landing fields are only about ten-foot square." "Do it up in a report, Dave," said Larry. "We'll turn it into a series of ads."

"That's not all," continued Forman. "In bitter winter weather, they're using these helicopters to take injured and ill men out to hospitals—a tremendous boost to morale. When they need a landing spot in an area that's all timber, they hover and use rifles to shoot the saplings down. Then they land, finish clearing, and build a complete camp. We've got movies of this."

The company accepted the fact that military and financial circles didn't take an immediate interest in the new product. "It's the young, spirited, pioneering types who hardly have any money. They're starting the helicopter businesses—men like Ham Reedy, who started the Chicago helicopter service," said Larry.

Larry and Forman had sold two hundred helicopters when the commercial market dried up completely in the spring of 1950. Larry had plans for another three hundred. He went to General Jacob L. Devers, commander of U.S. Army Ground Forces, equipped with movies, reports, and his own dynamic sales pitch. "I gave him a dose of helicopters," he said later.

But the military wasn't willing to accept the helicopter without changes and modifications. In one Pentagon session, Larry was told, "You ought to make your helicopter roadable; then it would be really versatile."

"Why roadable?"

"It could land in a pasture, shift gears, become an automobile, and then drive up the road to headquarters."

"General," said Larry, "that must be intended as a joke. It would be like putting wheels on a seagull. Why land in a pasture and drive to headquarters on a road? You don't need a road. You fly to headquarters and land at the front door."

Bell spent millions of dollars demonstrating the helicopter everywhere there seemed to be an interest. Test pilot Joe Mashman was assigned to the effort, moving from military base to base and flying day and night. His assignment: Take the officers for rides. Then take their wives and children, too. Give everybody a look at the helicopter.

Forman summed up the effort: "We weren't only trying to sell the helicopter to the military. We were trying to sell it to the world. And there was no other way to do it but to demonstrate it. We demonstrated all the time."

Some resistance to helicopters came from pilots. "A man

First airplane to fly indoors in the United States, the Bell experimental model No. 2 in Buffalo's 65th Regiment Armory on May 10, 1944. The pilot is Floyd Carlson.

Carlson takes Mayor LaGuardia for a ride and Larry shakes his hand. The New York Police Dept. ended up with Bell helicopters.

Floyd Carlson flies the Model 30 outside Bell's Gardenville, N.Y., workshop.

Model 30 takes shape.

Gen. Jacob J. Devers inspects a helicopter with the help of Dave Forman, Larry Bell, and Ray Whitman.

who can fly bombers and fighters thinks of himself as a pretty sharp flier. He looks at the helicopter with suspicion and reasons if *he* can't fly it, something must be wrong with it," said Bell.

When the Korean War broke out in June 1950, the army had before it Larry's proposal for a military production run of five hundred helicopters. He soon got the order, helicopters went into rescue service in Korea's rugged terrain, and the contracts for Bell helicopters came in a steady flow. Only a few changes were needed in the basic Bell commercial design, the 200 hp 47D-1, to adapt it for the army and marine troops in Korea.

Just before the war, Bell had announced development of skid landing gear for its helicopters. This was made of aluminum tubing and weighed less than half the standard wheels. Pilots were able to land on almost any type of rough or sloping terrain without the threat of tipping or rolling. Some evacuations were made from ridges or hilltops where there was so little space to operate that the pilots actually flew their helicopters on the ground, skids just touching the surface or held down by soldiers acting as human ballast.

With litters attached to the skids, each military helicopter could carry two seriously wounded men, two "walking wounded," and the pilot. Thousands of soldiers were evacuated to Mobile Army Surgical Hospitals (MASH) in this way.

Bell sales in 1951 were $82 million, more than double the 1950 total. Employment climbed to more than 10,000, up from the post World War II low of 1,861 in 1948. Larry was determined to make the improved level of business last. "Keep selling the helicopter to the public," he told Forman. "There'll be a lot of helicopter pilots coming back from Korea. They'll need help getting jobs."

Promoting the helicopter meant a long series of business trips for Larry and public relations director Fran Dunn. Once, at a dance in California following a helicopter demonstration, Larry discovered several of his old West Coast aviation cronies. He wanted to be sociable, however, and asked Mrs. Donald Douglas: "Would you like to dance?"

"Yes, thank you . . ."

"Fran," said Larry, turning to Dunn, "dance with Mrs. Douglas!"

Dunn recalled: "Larry kept me dancing all night, while he drank scotch and talked to his pals."

On September 17, 1952, a thirty-one-year-old test pilot named Elton J. Smith flew a 47D-1 from the heliport at Bell's new Helicopter Division near Fort Worth, Texas, to the front lawn of the Niagara Falls plant. It was a 1,217 mile nonstop world record achieved in twelve hours and fifty-seven minutes of flying.

Bell had moved the entire helicopter program to Texas to separate it from his other programs. "I want an organization that thinks helicopters morning, noon, and night," he told the directors. "We have a great variety of projects in Buffalo. The staff doesn't have time to give more than a lick and a promise to the helicopter."

He made an arrangement with the navy for the company to spend about $5 million for building the Texas plant in return for the loan of a variety of navy equipment needed to get production going. Selecting Texas was easy. As a result of his successful venture in Marietta, Bell liked the South. There were also these considerations: "Texas was far enough from Buffalo, but not too far. California was already a big airplane center, and I wanted to get someplace with a more pioneering spirit than either Buffalo or California."

As a natural overnight stop for coast-to-coast air travelers, Texas was also able to lure visitors who were mildly interested in helicopters but not interested enough to go a long way just to see a production line.

As always, there was confusion in opening a new plant. Bell enjoyed telling this story about a trip he made to Texas in the early days: "There was a parking lot at one end and a landing field at the other. When I got down there, they told me they planned to build the helicopters in a line headed toward the parking lot, then turn them around and bring them down the road to the airport. I told them: 'What the Hell's the sense of that? Why don't you turn the line around and have them come out where they belong?' And that's the way it is now."

Larry developed this sales pitch: "People must realize that the helicopter is the only vehicle of transportation in the world that's self-contained. If you buy a helicopter, you don't need to build a road, a harbor, a right of way, or an airport. You don't need anything. And if you take off in a helicopter, you can go in any direction of the compass, directly to your destination. You don't have to follow a road, you don't have to go to an airport, you just go where you want to go.

Hats off from a Texas farmer as a helicopter demonstrates crop dusting.

Larry congratulates pilot Elton Smith after his nonstop Fort Worth-to-Buffalo flight on September 9, 1952.

His health failing, Larry takes a ride near the front line in Korea.

In Korea, air rescue makes the helicopter indispensable for modern armies.

Helicopters do a flyby at the Niagara Falls plant. Larry's office is just behind the second-floor patio at right.

"When you get there, you can land on any kind of field. We have various kinds of landing gears. You can land on floats in the water or in snow, mud, or anywhere. There's no preparation necessary. The helicopter is self-contained, and it's the only vehicle of transportation that is.

"The trouble with automobiles is they're all alike. They're all oblong in shape, they all have a wheel on each corner, and they're limited in dimensions so they can only go on roads. Without roads, you don't go anywhere.

"A lot of people don't realize how cheap a helicopter is. The machine costs more than an automobile, but that's because they're made in lesser quantities. The trouble is, very few of us realize that, when you drive down the highway, every fifty feet of pavement you ride over costs as much as the car. So you buy the car very cheap out of your right-hand pocket, but it takes a lot of cash out of your left-hand pocket to build the road."

Late in the Korean War, Larry paid his own way to take a front-line look at how his helicopters were being used in combat. It pleased him to the end of his life that the machine bearing his name was useful in saving lives, not destroying them.

The daily routine with young army officers in Korea proved to be hard physical work for aging Larry Bell. He complained of pain across his chest, and an examination confirmed what tests had indicated years earlier: Larry had hypertensive cardiovascular disease. His blood pressure was 220/160. He was given medication and sent on his way to hustle and worry his last few years on earth.

After a speaking engagement in Buffalo after the Korean trip, Larry said he had gone to the war zone "because, in all my years in aircraft, I'd never been to the front." The sheer numbers of young fighting men made a deep impression on him. "I had dinner in a mess hall with twenty thousand airmen," he said. "And I remember the time when I personally knew every man in the air corps."

14

Piercing the
Sound Barrier

There stood Bob Woods, sawing the air with his hands, standing with Larry Bell, and making a short-of-breath sales pitch about an airplane that could fly faster than sound. "We're right on the brink of it, Larry," said Woods. "Now's the time to act."

"Who's working with you?" asked Bell.

"Major Kotcher at Wright Field and John Stack at NACA. These guys will get the job done. Kotcher and I would make a swell design team."

Bell offered Woods a cigarette, then lit one himself. "Let's go into my office," he said.

Woods outlined the history behind the supersonic airplane concept. Rapid growth of technology in the early years of World War II had steadily pushed forward the speed of airplanes.

"Remember when we paid a pilot to dive-test the P-39 at 620 mph?" asked Woods. "It raised a lot of questions, and they're not being answered. Yet more and more pilots are flying as fast as bullets."

It was December 19, 1943. The day before, a meeting had been held in Washington by the National Advisory Committee for Aeronautics to discuss jet propulsion in England. The audience included some of the best of America's engineers from the military, government, and industry. Led by John Stack and Bell design engineer Robert A. Wolf, the subject turned to the problems of high speed aircraft. The meeting transcript reported:

"Mr. Wolf emphasized that by using jet propulsion the opportunity was at hand to build a high-speed research airplane to provide needed aerodynamic information for aircraft manufacturers. This information is particularly needed for the high-speed range of flight that is now reached by conventional fighter aircraft in dives, but which may be attained by jet propulsion aircraft in level flight. The development and testing of this aircraft could ideally be handled by the National Advisory Committee of Aeronautics."

Much of John Stack's research career had been directed toward development of superior aircraft, and he had long realized that available wind tunnels could no longer provide the answers. He had been promoting the idea of a flying laboratory for many months.

Intelligence reports from Germany told that the ME-163, equipped with a rocket engine, was capable of 600 mph and that the ME-262, with twin jets, could do 527 mph. Bell and the U.S. Army Air Forces were testing the P-59, and the British were flying their single-engine jet airplane.

From the battle fronts, there were reports of aircraft breaking apart in power dives. Pilots spoke of a "sound barrier." Those who had come back alive from an encounter described frightful experiences—shock waves and loss of control. It was believed that to hit the sound barrier meant certain destruction, in the same way every wheel has an rpm barrier where it will fly apart.

After some discussion, Bell told Woods, "Bob, I personally believe in the need for this research. But here's what's going to happen when we try to sell the idea: Someone is going to say, 'What good is this airplane?' And being just good for research isn't enough. Not during the middle of a war."

"There's a whole lot more than research in this, Larry," said Woods. "Airplane technology is going to stand still until someone knocks down the barrier."

"I'll go along with that," said Bell.

With Bell's approval, a letter was sent to Dr. George W. Lewis, NACA's director of aeronautical research, on December 29, 1943, specifically suggesting the development of a high speed airplane.

"We feel that it would be very desirable to have such a high speed 'flying laboratory' developed and that much valuable information concerning compressibility and control problems, powerplant operation, etc., could be obtained if a properly integrated research program were set up about such a project and that it would be highly beneficial to all aircraft manufacturers who are developing really high speed aircraft."

The letter also stated: "It appears quite possible to construct a single engine aircraft based on available gas turbine jet power plants which will fly at speeds in level flights exceeding the critical Mach numbers of currently used types of wings."

Dr. Lewis expressed his interest, and by April 14, Bell had sent NACA a three-view drawing of the proposed airplane.

Jet propulsion in the United States at the time meant one airplane—the Bell P-59 equipped with General Electric engines. This aircraft was not especially fast. The prospect of building a research airplane using then-available jets was not appealing to government and military scientists, so the Bell proposal was tabled and began to gather dust.

The turning point came at a routine meeting of Bob Woods and Ezra Kotcher at Wright Field. Woods was still convinced the project should use kerosene-burning jet engines, of the type that would someday power airlines. Kotcher wanted to use rockets similar to those developed for the Space Age.

Kotcher disclosed that an American company was developing a turbo pump rocket that had 6,000 pounds of thrust and convinced Woods it was worth a try. "With that kind of power, we could certainly design a supersonic airplane," Woods remarked.

Early in December 1944, Bell and air force engineers met at the Niagara Falls plant to lay out tentative requirements for the new airplane, to be known as XS-1 (X for experimental, S for sonic). It would have to fly at a minimum of 800 mph for two to five minutes at 35,000 feet or higher and carry five hundred pounds of equipment to record flight data. It also could not differ greatly from conventional airplane design, in order to prove conventional design would be practical at transonic speeds. The Army Air Technical Service Command, on March 16, 1945, awarded a contract for three transonic/supersonic aircraft.

The initial design work by Woods and Kotcher grew to include hundreds of NACA, AAF, and Bell engineers. They patterned the XS-1 on the lines of the 50-caliber bullet and made it just about as rugged. The tiny airplane would weigh more than six tons fully fueled. The aluminum covering on the wings was to be machine tapered from a thickness of slightly more than half an inch at the fuselage to normal aircraft thickness at the tip.

In a technical paper on the project, chief engineer Bob Stanley and design engineer R. J. Sandstrom said the XS-1 pilot would have a machine "so sturdy that it is probable that the pilot would break before the machine. He [is being] given an aircraft so powerful that it is capable literally of climbing and accelerating (almost)* vertically. With the ability to shut off all power instantaneously and with the ability to conduct at least the early stages of supersonic flight during a climbing attitude the pilot's ability to retreat from danger at any instant should go a long way toward promoting the objectivity of his tests. The XS-1 can prove or disprove conclusively the feasibility of supersonic flight with aircraft as we know them."

Conventional wing design was used because information on the newer sweepback wings was too fragmentary. Its tail section was set high so it would not be affected by wing wake air. Since the XS-1 was to be so small, it used only standard, unpowered, pilot controls.

As the months passed, it became apparent that the original turborocket on which the project was based was not going to develop as expected. The problem was solved when the navy agreed to let the XS-1 use a 6,000 pound thrust rocket engine being built by Reaction Motors Inc. (RM) in New Jersey. This engine had four tubes, each delivering 1,500 pounds of thrust, and it burned alcohol and liquid oxygen, which were safe and easy to handle compared with the acid/aniline propellants of the original XS-1 engine.

The navy was sponsoring development of the RM engine for a high-speed airplane to be built by Douglas, the D-558-2. First flight tests of this aircraft were to be powered by jet engine, with rocket installation later, so the navy generously let the air force use the RM engine first in its XS-1.

Invented by James Wyld, the RM engine was the first rocket to be regeneratively cooled. It wouldn't overheat, a fault of many contemporary rockets, because its cold propellants flowed through the engine in built-in pipes to the combustion chambers.

The war was nearly over when Woods's engineering team

---

*Qualifier inserted by C. Yeager, 1976.

completed detail design of the XS-1. It was determined the aircraft was capable of withstanding 18g forces at 80,000 feet and 1,700 mph. Although originally intended to be flown from a landing strip, at Bob Stanley's suggestion a B-29 "mother" ship system was designed to launch the XS-1 at high altitude. This avoided the dangers of ground takeoff and saved fuel for high speed flight at high altitude. Stanley estimated that the potential speed and altitude would nearly double as a result of B-29 launching, since half the XS-1's fuel would be needed for ground takeoff and flight to high altitude.

Large numbers of B-29s became available at the end of World War II. The Army readily supplied a standard aircraft for the research program. The bomb doors were removed. Loading was achieved by lowering the XS-1 into a pit, moving the B-29 over it, and hoisting the research airplane to standard bomb shackles. An enclosed ladder was installed between the B-29 and the XS-1 so the pilot and flight personnel could go back and forth between the two airplanes while airborne.

Fuel for the XS-1 had become a problem because a turbo pump for the RM engine had not developed as expected. Waiting for it to be completed would delay the flight program, so it was decided to use a nitrogen pressure system to force propellants to the engine. The extra two thousand pounds added by the steel nitrogen tanks reduced by half the amount of fuel the XS-1 could carry. If it had not been for Stanley's B-29 mother ship idea, there would have been no powered flight test program until the turbo pump was delivered, several months later, when it was then installed on X-1 No. 3.

The XS-1 rolled out of the Niagara Falls plant just after Christmas, 1945. There was one "captive" flight attached to the B-29, without launch on January 10. Then the airplane was shipped to Pinecastle, Florida, where 10,000-foot runways were available and the weather was mild.

Test pilot Jack Woolams was the first man to fly the XS-1, glide testing it from an altitude of 27,000 feet. The flight took twelve minutes, and Woolams landed the aircraft on 3,000 feet of runway. "Larry," Bob Stanley told Bell by phone from the flying field, "we're in business. We've got a flying machine here."

The first flight was made with fuel tanks empty. Later, they were filled with water, which was jettisoned in flight to simulate what would happen in powered flight. A total of fourteen glide

The B-29 production line, January 1944.

Bell Aircraft's smallest and largest airplanes of World War II: XP-77 under the tail of a B-29.

A Bell B-29 takes off for combat service.

Bob Stanley with General Marshall at a P-59 demonstration.

The first two Bell X-airplanes in fabrication.

The four-barrelled Reaction Motors Inc. X-1 engine.

XS-1 in flight over Edwards Air Force Base, California.

Yeager enters the XS-1 for a ground test.

Chuck Yeager and his wife, Glennis, take a ride with Bell pilot Joe Cannon.

Yeager, tucked inside the XS-1's tiny cockpit, glances up into the mother ship before launch time. Courtesy L.A. Times

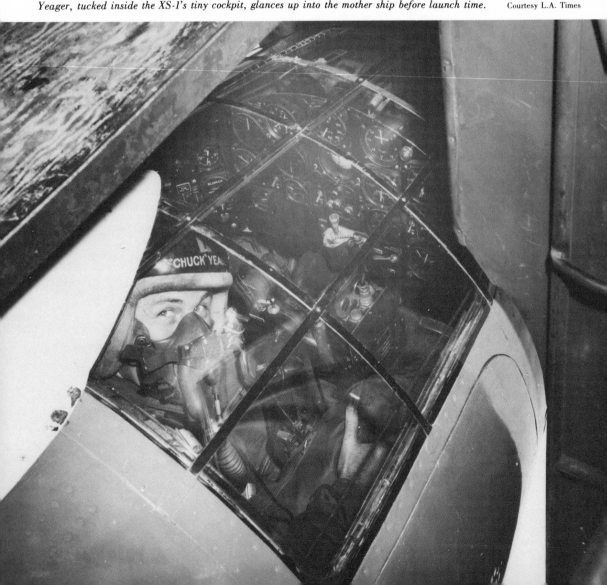

President Truman congratulates Collier Trophy winners Chuck Yeager and Larry Bell. The trophy is in the background.

Chuck Yeager, Capt. James T. Fitzgerald Jr. (X-1 pilot who later died in a P-80 crash), and Larry at the Bell Niagara Falls plant.

tests were made before the first RM engine was delivered on March 26 and flying stopped for engine installation.

Chalmers "Slick" Goodlin was the pilot on December 9, when the first powered flight was made over Muroc Dry Lake. The drop was normal. Ten seconds later, Goodlin ignited rocket chamber No. 1, giving him 1,500 pounds of thrust. Then he ignited chamber No. 2, and the aircraft began a steep climb, too steep, in Goodlin's estimation, so he shut down the second chamber and flew the XS-1 with 25 percent of its power to 35,000 feet. At that altitude, he re-ignited the second chamber and quickly reached Mach .795, then shut down both engines and glided to 15,000 feet.

Goodlin made one more test before landing. He turned on all four XS-1 rocket chambers. The aircraft seemed to leap forward—Goodlin later described it as similar to a water-injection takeoff of a piston driven fighter aircraft—and started another steep climb. Then Goodlin shut down again and glided to a landing.

A series of twenty similar tests, none of which exceeded Mach .8, eight-tenths the speed of sound, were made by Goodlin and chief test pilot Alvin M. "Tex" Johnston before the aircraft was turned over to the air force on June 2, 1947. Delivery of XS-1 No. 2 was made at the same time. The first phase of the project was finished. An air force press release announced:

"Bell Aircraft's contract called for demonstration of minimum performance requirements which included: First, an 8g pull-out at an indicated airspeed not exceeding 500 miles per hour . . . and flight with satisfactory control at a speed of .8 Mach."

The air force was still not claiming plans for supersonic flight: "It is expected that further flights of the XS-1 will be made to collect additional information about the way airplanes behave in the ranges approaching the speed of sound."

Newspapers made such conjectures as this, from the *Washington Evening Star*: "Beyond [the speed of sound] lies a no-man's land of turbulent aerodynamic forces uncharted even in the most advanced wind tunnels."

Later, Larry Bell described the manufacturer's approach to the XS-1: "One of the important things to consider with the engineers . . . is that they have had to be of an imaginative inclination and possessed of a mind not cluttered up with laws, formulas, and precedents applying to planes propelled by reciprocating engines. The first thing they had to do was throw away all the books which said 'you can't do this' or 'you can't do that.' After that, they were on their own.''

When Bell Aircraft turned the aircraft over to the air force, Colonel Albert Boyd, chief of the Flight Test Division, selected twenty-four-year-old Captain Charles E. Yeager as pilot. Yeager seemed an unlikely choice. He was a young man from the little community of Hamlin, West Virginia (pop. 850), who enlisted as a private in the U.S. Army Air Corps in 1941, immediately after high school graduation, and went to work as a mechanic. Two years later, at the height of the war, he won his appointment as a flight officer and was assigned to fly P-51s with the 363d Fighter Squadron.

Yeager built up a reputation for coolness in 270 combat hours, flying sixty-four missions and shooting down thirteen German airplanes. On his ninth mission, he was wounded in the leg and shot down by three Messerschmitts over occupied France.

The French underground smuggled him over the Spanish border where he was jailed, but his jailers failed to take away his emergency kit, which contained a small highly tempered saw. The bars were brass, so Yeager was free the same night, and in a short time the British were able to get him to England. Sent home in February 1945, he immediately married the girl he had left behind in 1943, Glennis Fay Dickhaust, of Oroville, California. After working as a flight instructor for a short time, he won an assignment to Wright Field as a test pilot.

Colonel Boyd knew his men well. He needed a flyer who would methodically and carefully pilot a flying laboratory into the unknown. Several of his pilots had extensive engineering training and held degrees, but Yeager came up with the assignment. It was a "gut" decision by Colonel Boyd.

After the young pilot completed his first unpowered flights, the engineers sensed he was perfect for the job. "Charlie Yeager is completely nerveless," said Richard H. Frost, Bell pilot-project engineer. "He's the coolest guy I've ever seen, and it's been my business to see a lot of pilots preparing for flights of doubtful outcome. He is a perfectly natural airman, if there is such a thing. He flies a plane as though it were a part of him. In his test work, he does exactly what the aeronautical engineers request, and he brings back the answers."

On his first powered flight, however, the young captain

showed a pioneering streak. Against instructions, he took the aircraft to a speed that stunned the control crew.

Yeager had become a veteran at gliding the XS-1 by August 29, 1947, when he was given his first opportunity to turn on the power. The test plan called for him to ignite the four thrust chambers one at a time until he reached Mach .8, then cut power and glide to earth. As always, the worst part of the trip for Yeager was the climb down the tiny ladder from the B-29 bomb bay through the frigid blast of high altitude air to the frozen seat in the open cockpit of the X-1. He always disliked that ordeal, but inside, with the door secure, it was something else. Chuck Yeager in a cockpit was in a world where he was master.

The young rocket pilot heard a four-three-two-one count down, as the seconds approached for the bomb racks to let him go. The drop was at 20,000 feet. Yeager performed a single-chamber rocket test, as called for in the flight card, then glided silently to 5,000 feet before reigniting the engine. Against instructions, he almost instantly pushed the buttons for all four rocket chambers and the airplane jumped into a near vertical climb to 30,000 feet. The Mach meter read .85 when Yeager cut the engine and made the flight back to Muroc, mentally preparing the explanation for his behavior. "I might have been a little rapid touching off those chambers," he said. Among his superiors there was some show of consternation. Privately, they were delighted that the first power-on air force flight had topped twenty-one previous powered flights.

The push was on. Yeager was flying or briefing constantly as the program steadily edged the engine-on time upward toward the thrust needed for Mach 1 flight. There were no more deviations from the plan by Captain Yeager. He lived up to his reputation for stability, hard work, and discipline as the flight program entered the speed range where the XS-1 was severely buffeted and sometimes strangely dipped to the right. There also were times when the airplane seemed to move through the air like a high speed porpoise, bobbing nose up, nose down. None of it shook Yeager's confidence. "Let's go," he'd tell the engineers. "Let's get at it."

Tuesday, October 14, 1947, was set as the date for the first try for sonic speed. On the preceding Friday, the aircraft had been made ready, and there was one final briefing late in the day. The complete flight crew was present—Captain Jack Ridley, project engineer, and flight surgeon Major John P.

Stapp, who made up the B-29 launch team. The two P-80 chase pilots were also present: First Lieutenant Robert A. Hoover, who was alternate XS-1 pilot, and Richard Frost of Bell. The briefing was long and intense.

"Now let's enjoy the weekend," said Captain Ridley as the meeting ended.

Yeager relaxed as hard as he worked. Saturday night, he and Glennis went out for dinner at Pancho Barnes' Dude Ranch. There were martinis, dinner wine, and after-dinner drinks. Then they decided a late-night horseback ride would be a perfect way to end the evening.

The desert air was exhilarating, and the sky was thick with stars. "Race you back to the corral," Chuck shouted to Glennis, turning his horse swiftly. He was yards ahead, but someone had shut the gate. Yeager's horse raced into it throwing him to the ground. As he dusted himself off, Glennis jumped off her horse and ran to him. "It was nothing. I'm all right," Chuck said. But as he drove home, Glennis noticed he seemed to have trouble breathing.

"You're in pain, Chuck. You'd better see a doctor."

Yeager well realized that the long hours of work toward the first sonic flight would suffer a setback if he went to flight surgeon Stapp or the base doctor. They would almost certainly ground him. On Sunday, Yeager found a civilian doctor. The diagnosis: Two broken ribs. He asked the doctor to tape up his chest and told no one about the injury. "A couple of cracked ribs has got nothing to do with this flight," he told Glennis that night. "I'm not running this race; I'm flying it."

On Tuesday, the B-29 climbed 20,000 feet and was doing 250 mph when it dropped the XS-1 at 10:26 A.M. Yeager glided down away from the bomber and fired the rocket chambers. The tiny airplane climbed rapidly past 40,000 feet; and Yeager leveled off, letting the full 6,000 pounds of thrust push the aircraft in level flight. There was some roughness and buffeting, but it subsided as Chuck watched the Mach meter closely. The needle reached .98. It wavered, then went off the scale, past Mach 1. For a moment, every nerve in Yeager's body was ready to respond to the expected violent reaction that seemed certain to greet this step into the unknown. Then he relaxed and flew a smooth supersonic flight.

"Good Lord," Yeager thought as he glided back to Muroc. "There *is* no barrier."

That afternoon, the instruments confirmed the result of the

test: Yeager had reached Mach 1.06, 700 mph, at 43,000 feet. He was the first supersonic man. But on the ground, he winced when someone slapped his back. Flight surgeon Stapp noticed the pained expression and soon had Yeager in his office, stripped to the waist. The surgeon was silent as he examined the cracked ribs and later told only a few of his superiors about the incident. No one ever spoke of it again.

On November 11, more than a month after the flight, *Aviation Week* magazine reported progress of the Douglas Skyrocket which "combines the rocket power of the XS-1 with the turbojet power of the Chance Vought Pirate," then added: "Navy, Douglas and NACA engineers are confident that sonic speed with a piloted aircraft is now only a question of getting the D-558-2 into the air and striking for the mark."

There were some air force smiles at Edwards and in Larry Bell's office over that sentence, but strict silence blanketed the historic flight. But the story was too big to keep secret. *Aviation Week* was the first to break the news in its December 22 edition. It was one of the biggest scoops in the magazine's history, and it raised a furor in the air force and the Department of Defense.

Time magazine summed it up on January 5, 1948*: "It was the longest step in aeronautical development since Orville Wright first flew at Kitty Hawk, N.C., forty-four years ago. But the air force's pride of achievement was dulled by the fact that it had not succeeded in guarding the secret of basic aerodynamic design which had opened up the supersonic speed zone. The air force could and did keep secret the speeds which had been attained in its epoch-making flight.

"The air force told its official story after *Aviation Week*, a fortnight ago, published an account of the XS-1's straight-wing design; the air force had unwarily released them twelve months ago. Much U.S. supersonic research—and presumably that of other nations—had been centered on a swept-back design. The effect of publication was to tell all the other nations and potential enemies: Forget the swept-back design; as of now, at least, the straight wing is it."

In an editorial, the *Washington Post* said, "If, as the magazine's editors contend, the air force had been preparing a

*Reprinted by permission of *TIME, The Weekly News Magazine*; copyright Time, Inc., 1948.

release of its own on this accomplishment in breaching the supersonic wall, then all the subsequent fuss is meaningless."

That December 17, President Truman awarded the Collier Trophy to Larry Bell, John Stack, and Chuck Yeager* for their parts in the XS-1 program. Before the Aero Club of Washington that night, Larry paid special tribute to the memory of Jack Woolams, first XS-1 pilot, and Captain James T. Fitzgerald, Jr., who flew the aircraft beyond the speed of sound on his first flight and then was killed in a P-80 crash later in 1948.

Bell mentioned several of the engineers: Kotcher, Woods, Stanley Smith (Bell project manager), and Dick Frost, and then described some of the achievements made by the engineers: "Due to the high speeds and high altitudes at which the X-1 was intended to operate, many problems were presented. Because of the lack of needed apparatus, much improvising was necessary to accomplish the desired results. As an example, there was not in existence any type of fuel pump that could pump liquid oxygen at 360 degrees below zero, Fahrenheit, and alcohol and water at the required high capacity. This necessitated an improvised fuel system, which by its very nature reduced the airplane's fuel capacity. This fuel system involved twelve specially constructed steel spherical bottles ranging from fifteen to twenty-one inches in diameter to be connected together and tucked away in the odd corners of the limited space available in the airplane. These bottles carried inert gases under pressure of 4,500 pounds per square inch. Inasmuch as commercial nitrogen gas could not be obtained in excess of 2,000 pounds pressure, it was necessary to develop and build special nitrogen evaporators to produce gas at the desired high pressure.

"Many accessories suitable for this project were unavailable. There existed no air speed indicators or Mach meters to measure the high speeds expected. There was no altimeter that would register the airplane's expected altitude. It was too hazardous for the pilot to attempt to fly at these speeds and altitudes without these direct reading instruments.

---

*In its April 18, 1948 issue, *Time* magazine reported, "Goodlin was offered a fat reward (a rumored $150,000) for flying it at full speed, but he did not like the terms. Another civilian pilot had a try at the X-1 and hastily bowed out. Then the air force took charge and gave the job to Chuck Yeager, who did it in line of duty for a captain's salary ($511.50 a month, including flying pay and extras)." (Reprinted by permission of *TIME, The Weekly News Magazine*; copyright Time, Inc., 1949.)

"While the X-1 was designed to take off under its own power on its own landing gear, it has always been launched by dropping from the belly of a B-29 at high altitude. This procedure came about by happenstance. After the airplane was completed, its initial flight tests were delayed six months awaiting certain accessories. It was then that our engineers conceived the idea of dropping it from a B-29 at high altitude as a glider in order to give the pilot an opportunity to determine the flying characteristics of the airplane. Jack Woolams, in the winter of 1946, made twelve such drops in Florida, where there was available a 10,000 foot runway. These twelve ten-minute glide familiarization flights determined the stalling speed and the flying characteristics of the airplane. In fact, it worked so well that the procedure has since been adopted for use with full fuel aboard, as it completely eliminates all take-off hazard of the heavily loaded airplane. In the event the rocket engine fails to start, all fuel can be expelled by the high pressure blow-out system, permitting landing always in light condition.

"Perhaps the most significant thing about the X-1 is the fact that the airplane has been flown many, many times in the subsonic, transonic, and supersonic ranges of speeds in its original configuration as it came off the drawing boards, and not a single change has ever been made or now deemed necessary. A real tribute to the engineers responsible."

It wasn't the last word on the subject. Yeager recalled hearing an air force general remark, "Someday, Larry Bell is going to walk into this office and exclaim, 'We want to fly to the moon.' If I am still here, I will undoubtedly say, 'Larry, get started on it. If anyone can do it, you and your company can!'"

Air Force, civilian, and NASA pilots flew the X-1. The complete list is as follows: Chalmers (Slick) Goodlin; Robert A. Hoover; Captain Charles E. Yeager; Jack Woolams; Joe Cannon; Alvin E. (Tex) Johnston; Jean (Skip) Ziegler; Howard C. Lilly; Scott Crossfield; John Griffin; Robert A. Champine; John B. McKay; Major General Albert Boyd; Colonel Jackie Ridley; Lieutenant Colonel Gus Askounis; Lieutenant Colonel Frank K. Everest, Jr.; Lieutenant Colonel Richard L. Johnston; Lieutenant Colonel P. D. Fleming; Major Gus Lundquist; and Captain James Fitzgerald.

15

World
Without War

Production collapsed at Bell Aircraft in the days before Japan surrendered, August 14, 1945. The huge work force of men and women seemed jubilant. There was laughter among the unfinished airplanes on halted production lines. There were kisses and tears and pledges that friendships forged in war would be preserved forever. But the Termination Office was working overtime sending bankers back to banking and women riveters back to the kitchen.

The winding down of the Niagara Frontier Division was gradual, compared to Georgia where, of 26,514 persons on the payroll that August, only 92 were left by September 30. In Buffalo, the need for fighter aircraft had declined gradually. Employment at the Niagara Frontier had dropped from 28,325, in early 1944, to 19,264, a year later, and to 5,326 by the end of June, 1945.

Bell stayed in business in Buffalo and Burlington, but the government-owned facility at Marietta was moth-balled. After the V-J Day contract cancellations, the company had only $34 million in business backlog compared with a backlog of more than $500 million at the beginning of that year.

After the war, Larry had no patience with the trappings of better times. He moved out of his oak-paneled office and went out into the open, working from a gray desk just across from the cashier's cage. Larry and Irene Bernhardt sat in full view behind the glass windows of Larry's "hard times" office.

What was left of Bell Aircraft had the elements of almost

certain postwar success. Larry's willingness to go into new and advanced fields had made his company more versatile than other aircraft builders:

—The X-series supersonic aircraft program had made a solid start.
—Bell was developing what would become a very successful line of helicopters.
—The Tarzon gyro-stabilized bomb program (first of what would become known as "smart" bombs) had been brought from the Georgia plant to Niagara Falls.
—The army had requested a proposal for an air-to-ground guided missile that would eventually become the Bell Rascal missile program.
—A capability for electronics had been developed because of the company's work with radio controls for the P-59. By early 1946, Bell would develop radio control equipment for the P-80, and much more electronic work would follow.

Larry summarized his views on October 10, 1945, before a Senate committee investigating the national defense program: "During the war, the aviation industry developed a technique for producing aircraft in very large quantities and at a rapid tempo. But production programs and research programs should be very carefully balanced, and aircraft production should at all times be based on the most advanced engineering and research of which we are capable.

"Some of the most remarkable aviation developments of the war—for example, the entire jet propulsion and rocket program, the German V-weapons, radar, and atomic bomb—were important instruments of warfare based on research and development. It will be noted that these developments were not exclusively our own. At the close of the war, the opposing forces were engaged in a scientific race, and it was a close race.

"It is my own impression, based on a recent trip to Germany some weeks ago, that the Germans were ahead of us in some respects, and that they might have been even farther ahead if their war lords had not made a series of unintelligent policy decisions as to the use of their newer devices.

"We may depend on it, I believe, that other nations, friendly or unfriendly, will spare no efforts to keep up their scientific development programs, and it would seem clear that we must match this effort if we are to be secure. For, despite the rapid advances made recently, many other dramatic developments in aircraft are just over the horizon. . . ."

Larry traveled coast to coast in the search for business after the war. On one trip to see Donald Douglas in California, Fran Dunn noticed Larry had begun to act fidgety as the train neared Kansas City. "Check the luggage into a hotel," Larry told Dunn. "I'll meet you there."

When twenty-four hours passed with no word from Larry, Dunn phoned his office, then Larry's. Nobody knew Bell's whereabouts. "What'm I supposed to do?" Dunn asked Bell's secretary, Irene.

"Better stay put."

A day later, Larry showed up. "Let's get going. We're late," he said.

There was not a word about what Larry had been doing for two days and two nights, but Dunn had long experience in traveling with Larry Bell. "Larry had intimate friends in a lot of cities," Dunn later recalled.

The company tried for additional sales of the P-59 and a faster jet, the XP-83, which was capable of Mach .72. But only two prototype XP-83s were built, and the P-59 was already outdated. Although Bell Aircraft would win fame as a developer of advanced concepts, other companies were always to win the big aircraft production contracts.

In the summer of 1945, the army had delivered to the Georgia Division a prototype "smart bomb" built by the Gulf Research Corporation and gave Bell a contract to build ten additional bombs. The program was brought to Niagara Falls when the war ended.

The "Tarzon Bomb" had a rudder and elevator controlled by radio, and four ailerons that were gyro-stabilized by pneumatic controls. It could be steered to the target and deliver a 6,700-pound warhead with great accuracy.

While Niagara Falls developed the Tarzon, in Vermont the Ordnance Division (later to be renamed the Burlington Division) became a bright spot for commercial production. With fewer than two thousand employees and headed by a veteran administrator, Julius J. Domonkos, Burlington won a large contract from Kaiser-Fraser's Graham-Paige Motors Corporation and went to work building 5-horsepower, two-cycle engines and transmissions for a new line of garden roto-tillers.

The division attained a high volume of production and was

Rascal missile is launched from a B-50.

The last Bell fighter P-63 rolls off the production line, April 1945.

A lineup of P-63s in 1945. From the top, an armored RP-63 used for gunnery practice, a French-painted model, a Soviet and a U.S.A.F. plane.

First of the "smart" bombs, the Bell Tarzon.

Bell XP-83, the big jet fighter intended for postwar service. Only two prototypes were built.

The General Electric/Whittle jet engine.

making a good profit when Graham-Paige had to stop roto-tiller production because of a strike elsewhere. The Burlington contract was cancelled with about half of the original order for eighty thousand engines built.

Without that order, Bell's division didn't have enough business to stay open, so Larry wired Graham-Paige to live up to its contract. There was no reply, and Bell wired Kaiser-Fraser demanding a conference the next day, "in my office." Later, Bell recalled: "So the next morning, by golly, Fraser was in my office. . . . He said the situation was different from anything he had encountered before 'because he was an automobile man.' Fraser told me, 'I read your contract very carefully yesterday, and if you hadn't written it just the way you did, why, it would be your problem. You'd have to get out of this the best you could. But I find the contract pretty binding.' 'I know it is,' I said."

As a settlement, Bell ended up with a note covered by Kaiser-Fraser stock as security. "We had the controlling interest in Kaiser-Fraser Company until they paid that note. But we wouldn't have gotten that if we hadn't had a good contract. A little Yankee up in Burlington was our lawyer, and he was a pretty smart contract writer. He wrote a good one," Bell recalled.

Bell shut down the Burlington plant and brought its key people to Buffalo. After some dickering with General Electric, which knew what Bell had paid for it ($600,000), he sold it to them for $1.5 million.

Commercial business appealed to Bell, and he asked his staff to suggest applications for a small horsepower engine. Rather than subcontract, why not develop a complete product based on the company's capability to turn out inexpensive engines? A meeting was held in Bell's office to review the results of the survey. He was dissatisfied. "Lawnmowers, scooters, farm implements—these fields are too crowded," said Bell. "Hasn't anyone got a likely product?"

There was silence as Bell looked around the room.

"Well," he said, "we're going to put a small engine on something, even if it's a wheelbarrow!"

Larry's face brightened. "A wheelbarrow. That's it. A wheelbarrow! The only improvement in ten thousand years of wheelbarrows has been a rubber tire!"

The next morning, one of the world's finest teams of missile and aircraft engineers went to work on the wheelbarrow. They made some interesting discoveries as they produced what would be known as the Bell Prime Mover motorized wheelbarrow patented in the name of Larry Bell. "This rugged and versatile machine carries a half-ton load of raw or finished goods almost anywhere a man can walk, uphill or down, indoors or out, over rough or smooth ground," the company claimed. "It plows snow, moves earth, supplies auxiliary power. The almost infinite uses for this product increase productivity of common labor several times and on many jobs can return the original cost to the owner within a period of several weeks."

The Prime Mover had a self-dumping bucket and dragged a steel platform so the operator wouldn't have to walk. "An old man can work all day and not even breathe hard," said Bell. Its payload was five times the two hundred pound load a man can carry in a wheelbarrow.

There was some kidding on the golf courses about the pioneering aviation company now engaged in pioneering such an earth-bound device. "That's perfectly all right with me," said Bell. "Talk all you want. It helps sell more wheelbarrows."

Government business was Larry's first love, however. Bell returned to the Senate defense subcommittee a second time in 1946 and recommended that the nation continue to support development of military aircraft "in sufficient volume to permit us to keep together a small but highly skilled group of scientists, technicians, engineers, and other necessary personnel with high skills. That would be the minimum. Such highly skilled and technical personnel must work together as a team, and such a team must have at least enough work to keep it functioning steadily and efficiently."

At home, Lucille and Larry treated each other with affection but spent more and more time apart. On May 15, 1948, the couple filed separation papers and made a property settlement "in view of their intention to live separate and apart for the rest of their natural lives." Lucille later obtained a divorce and remarried.

(Lucille died on December 10, 1970. At the time of her death she was married to the former U.S. Senator from Connecticut, Archibald McNeil, and had spent her last years living in Palm Beach, Florida.)

About a year before Hap Arnold's death in 1950, Bell visited

Harry Truman's last defense plant inspection as vice president was made at Bell Aircraft Corporation. Later the same day a dinner with business and community leaders was held in the Buffalo Country Club. (Senator James Mead was ill and unable to attend the event on April 9, 1945.) Not long thereafter, President Roosevelt had died and Truman was living at a new address, but he didn't seem very excited about it.

THE WHITE HOUSE
WASHINGTON

April 13, 1945

Dear Mr. Bell:

Appreciated most highly your cordial note of April Ninth.

I enjoyed the visit to your plant immensely and am certainly glad I had a chance to pay that visit. I also enjoyed the visit to the Country Club.

I hope Jim Mead is fully recovered by now.

Circumstances have certainly altered since I saw the Buffalo crowd.

Sincerely yours,

Harry Truman

Mr. Lawrence D. Bell
2050 Elmwood Avenue
Buffalo, New York

Vice President Harry S Truman with Larry on April 8, 1945, a few days before Truman became president.

Larry's home in Eggertsville, near Buffalo, before he and Lucille separated and he moved into an apartment.

Larry in his office, 1947.

him at his home in Sonoma, California. Arnold held the highest rank in the service—five-star general of the air force. Through his efforts, the air force had achieved parity with the army and navy through the National Defense Act of 1947. The struggles had been hard, and the two men spent long hours reminiscing.

Bell's mind was "running wild on bacteria"; Bell asked Arnold if he knew of recent developments in bacteriological warfare. General Arnold pointed to a half-empty water glass on the table. "Larry, this much bacteria would kill everybody in New York City."

Later, Bell recalled, "That was his remark. It was made in such a way that he showed he was just as fearful of bacteria as I am. I think, compared to bacteria, guided missiles and airplanes are hardly a threat. There are so many kinds of bacteria. It can be worked so that all the animals die. There are chemicals or bacteria that can be delivered by guided missiles at high altitudes over the land to kill the crops. There are insects that can be dropped which breed overnight, and you're sunk with insects."

Bell complained to Arnold about a trend in the military services away from personal leadership. "I don't know who to talk to anymore," said Bell. "It used to be I could call Washington and talk to somebody, but now everything's run by committee. You can't get anything done."

In the months after the war, the battle for business was only one of the challenges faced by Larry Bell. UAW Local 501, which had not once struck the company from the time it was organized in 1937, called a one-day strike over grievances in late 1945. And there was talk that some leaders of the local were Communists. Trouble was brewing.

In New York City, a group of financiers looked at the troubled company as a large pile of cash. They were right. At war's end, Bell had little else but money. Most of its facilities were either government owned or leased. Powerful forces on Wall Street held the opinion that companies like Bell should liquidate and let what was left of the peacetime airplane business go to a few remaining companies. Then, to make Bell even more tempting, the company's stock fell below book value because of its lack of business.

Battle lines with the union and with the financiers were slowly taking shape as Bell Aircraft struggled to stay alive in the second half of the 1940s.

16

Battle of
the Proxies

Applause thundered in Kleinhans Music Hall at the announcement: "Chancellor's Medal of the University of Buffalo awarded to Lawrence Dale Bell." Larry walked stiffly to the rostrum and shook hands with Chancellor Samuel P. Capen, who sensed Bell's uneasiness at the continuing applause. "It's your community paying tribute to you," said Capen.

The ceremony went smoothly. Larry Bell, the vocational high school dropout who hadn't sat in a classroom for thirty-five years, eloquently accepted one more in a long line of honors from the academic world. But on this day, there was bitter irony. Praised as the "inspiring director of thousands" who had "dignified Buffalo in the eyes of the world," Larry was on the brink of losing his job and his factory in February 1947.

For nearly a year, a group of dissident shareholders led by Jackson Martindell and Edward R. Stettinius, Jr., of New York City, had been gathering Bell common stock in a campaign against Larry's control of his company. Their reasoning: Bell Aircraft had very little work for the huge Niagara Falls plant, yet the company had $31.6 million in assets and only $12.8 million in liabilities. There were 434,789 shares outstanding at a price of about $17.50 per share. A payoff of nearly $19 million was available if the company would liquidate.

"John, these sharks want to destroy everything we've built," Larry told a key director, John L. Bierwirth, as the battle took shape. "Will you stick with me?"

"We're all with you," said Bierwirth.

Larry was haunted by the specter of failure. He had risen to the top of his profession, building a giant wartime company that had earned a good reputation. But though he did more than $1 billion in business, he had not become wealthy. Other than his investments in the company and some property—including a four-unit apartment house at 810 20th Street in Santa Monica—Larry had spent his earnings freely. Larry's private life, including liquor used for entertaining at home, came out of his salary. The factory was never asked to do a job for the president. "If I do it, how can I tell anyone else not to?" he had replied gruffly when someone asked if he might have a small aluminum household fixture made in the factory shop.

He felt the attack by Martindell's group was traitorous. After dinner with his closest associates late one night, he said, "After all this, I'm not going to die broke."

The fear of losing his job led Larry into making a tactical error that hurt his cause. He arranged through his board of directors to receive:

—A five-year employment contract at $55,000 minimum annually;

—A $160,000 annuity which would add some $10,000 to his $18,000-a-year pension he was scheduled to receive at age sixty, seven years later.

—$5 per unit sold after the first five thousand Prime Movers.

—A stock option plan in which Larry could buy up to 50,000 shares at prices that could range as low as half the market value.

Martindell's "shareholder committee," which saw every expenditure as money out of its pockets, attacked the proposals and belittled the board of directors that awarded them.

Earlier, Larry's purchases of the Niagara Falls and Vermont plants had infuriated the same shareholders. The Burlington plant and fourteen acres was a bargain at $600,000. The Niagara Falls plant and ninety-five acres cost only $4.3 million. But, by spending this sizable sum from the net worth, Larry had asserted his intention to stay in business. He was asking shareholders to be patient until the company once again began bringing in a profit.

The Martindell group suddenly announced that it intended to nominate a majority of directors in opposition to the incumbent board and implied that it had the necessary votes. "Manage-

ment proposes to pay [Larry Bell] $237,000 in 1947 irrespective
of earnings," said Martindell, who claimed the support of more
than forty thousand shares of stock, 11 percent of the total.

Larry countered that the statement was "completely inac-
curate." He said his salary was $55,000, reduced from $100,000
at his own request, "and I expect to receive no other compen-
sation during 1947."

The *Buffalo Evening News* reported that Martindell's shareholders committee had "put to work twenty persons in New
York City to solicit votes from the twenty-two hundred shareholders" and reported that if the seven Wall Street directors
were elected it would "probably mean Mr. Bell would be out as
head of the company."

In an effort to counter the attack, Larry's board withdrew
Larry's stock option plan. "The board apparently now recog-
nizes that its action in voting extravagant benefits for the presi-
dent of the corporation was indefensible," said Martindell.
"This board of directors was interested in taking care of Larry
Bell. Larry Bell is the victim of loving kindness."

Through proxies mailed to shareholders, the committee
proposed the following new directors: Stettinius, Martindell,
Benjamin Graham, Peter Berkey, C. W. Pearson, Stanley M.
Rowe, and M. T. Siberling. They intended to oust all but the
four original management representatives, Bell, Beard, Whitman, and Woods.

Bell management was at work on a campaign to keep the
incumbent board of directors. In addition to Larry, Bierwirth,
Beard, Whitman, and Woods, they were Charles Criqui, John
W. de Forest, Frederick F. Robinson, Ansley W. Sawyer, J. F.
Schoellkopf, Jr., and Walter Yates.

Larry used Harvey Gaylord's investment experience by
sending him to Wall Street. It was like starting the company
again, going out on the street after support. Once again, Bell
had little to offer except past performance and a promise for
the future.

Larry was more nervous than usual one blustery evening
when he and public relations director Fran Dunn boarded an
airplane for New York. The engines were warming up when
Larry suddenly unbuckled his seat belt and started toward the
front. His face was stark white.

"What're you doing, Larry?" asked Dunn.

"I can't go on this plane," said Bell. "See you there."

Bell joined Dunn the next day, and neither mentioned the incident again. Larry had once again displayed his fear of airplanes.

Sales at Bell Aircraft in 1946 totaled $11.5 million, and the loss for the year was $657,900. Bell's Model 47 helicopter had been licensed for commercial sales. It looked like a good source of future income, but there were no guarantees. Deliveries of Model 47s began just before January 1. By February 28, sales mounted to $1.3 million. The company informed shareholders that "all unfilled commercial helicopter orders are accompanied by substantial down payments."

The heart of the battle was in New York City. Large numbers of shares were held in "street name" by the Wall Street brokers. It meant the stocks were in the name of the brokerage houses but would be voted according to the wishes of the clients. The idea was to get the brokers to influence their clients.

The two sides bombarded shareholders with proxies and fought it out in the press. Larry and his friends owned a modest amount of shares, but nowhere near the 217,395 that would be needed to win a majority. Larry personally had 13,200 shares, Whitman had 4,067, and Ansley Sawyer had 1,804. The fight meant telephoning an endless number of shareholders from coast to coast.

Then, as the campaign neared the end, the telephone company went on strike. Larry was at his desk when the news came. He seemed to swell like salt-rising bread. "Get me the manager of the phone office," he shouted to Irene. The resulting conversation produced phenomenal service. Telephone supervisors kept Bell's lines open twenty-four hours a day.

As the deadline for the proxy count approached, Martindell admitted to reporters that some of his associates had talked to Larry about the possibility of a merger with Lockheed, at Lockheed's request. Asked if Larry would be retained by the shareholder committee's slate of directors, Martindell said: "Larry Bell is a friend of mine. But there are certain things when you are in business that you can't allow to be done to the shareholders." He denied any intent to liquidate.

A prominent group of Buffalo executives entered the fight with a letter to shareholders urging support of Bell management and expressing disagreement with Martindell's group. Then the chambers of commerce of Buffalo and Niagara Falls expressed their support, noting that the loss of Bell Aircraft would mean the end of the aircraft industry on the Niagara Frontier. This was an unhappy possibility to the thousands of former aircraft workers who had been employed at Bell, Curtiss-Wright, Consolidated, and the smaller western New York airplane companies in years past.

On the day of the annual meeting, April 22, 1947, Bell helicopters dramatically arrived on the front lawn of the plant with huge boxes of last-minute proxies. One box had been flown from New York City, then transferred to a helicopter at the Buffalo airport and speeded north to the plant. A helicopter got another box from a mail truck that had already started out from the post office in Buffalo. Nothing was spared to get all favorable proxies in by the deadline, 6:00 P.M. Monday, April 21, 1947.

Martindell's efforts were far less spectacular. He arrived on an early morning flight boasting that he was armed with more than thirteen hundred of the twenty-four hundred shareholder proxies.

There were reports that "undisclosed interests may be operating in the background" of Bell's management's opposition. The implication again was that Lockheed or some other major company that wanted the Bell facilities was maneuvering behind the scenes.

Larry went before the work force with a pep talk, promising that "if they want a battle, we'll give them a good one."

The opposing forces came together at 2:00 P.M. in the Frontier Room. All last-minute negotiations for peace had been swept aside, and the atmosphere was tense in the room packed with more than fifty shareholders, executives, lawyers, directors, and reporters.

Shareholder Lewis G. Harriman called for the re-election of the incumbent directors, and B. R. Bryant submitted the opposition slate. The opening session lasted only twenty minutes. The name of the winner was locked up in the boxes of proxies, and everyone was anxious to get the tally started. There were two general rules:

1. If a shareholder had signed more than one proxy, only the one with the latest postmark would be counted.

2. If there was any question by either side, that proxy would be thrown into a separate pile which would be counted only if it could change the result of the election.

At the start, one New York attorney expressed haughty

disbelief that an important Wall Street brokerage house had
signed a proxy for Bell management after earlier signing for
Martindell. "This one's in question," he said, tossing the proxy
aside.

Bell attorney Mason Damon gave him a thoughtful look and a
few minutes later did the same thing with a Martindell proxy for
an even larger number of shares. The New Yorker protested.
"Two can play the game," said Damon.

As the count continued, the teams were surprised to find that
a large number of shareholders had signed and mailed everything that was sent to them. Bell management had sent out
three proxies and the Martindell group sent four. The problem
was to sort them out and find the one with the latest postmark.

Management's effort to get the largest possible number of
last-minute proxies was showing success. Proxies from as far
away as Tyler, Texas, had been signed only a few hours earlier
and delivered by helicopter to the front door.

At sunset, Larry had the lights turned on throughout the
administration building so the visitors could walk the halls
rather than being trapped in the executive offices. Coffee was
served from the Frontier Room kitchen.

Reporters and shareholders wandered outside to look at the
grounds. Bob Watson of the *News* walked over to the dimly
lighted gate house for a few minutes, quietly examining the
brilliantly-illuminated main building.

"The tension in there's thicker'n fudge," he said to the
watchman.

"I got my money on Larry Bell," was the reply.

It was nearly twelve hours before the meeting resumed at
1:30 A.M. As Bell management took seats in the front, their
tenseness gave way to smiles. Larry had winked.

The election inspectors made their report: Bell management
was the winner, 207,936 to 140,751. The margin was great
enough to leave uncounted the 15,612 shares represented by
proxies in the disputed pile. Larry remained calm as the vote
was read, but the room erupted as the winners let go a cheer.
Supporters embraced Bell and shook his hand, and Larry's
face broadened into a wide grin.

The meeting was quickly resumed by Ray Whitman, who conducted a vote formally accepting the election results. In the back
of the room, Martindell stood up and said, almost inaudibly, that

Victory party on April 22, 1947, when Larry and his friends won the proxy fight. From left, Walter A. Yates, Bob Woods, Charles Criqui, Ansley Sawyer, and Larry Bell.

April 22, 1947: Larry goes before the Bell work force with the story of the proxy victory and plans for the future.

he wished the new board well, and would give them his cooperation. He was gone a few minutes later.

Bell told reporters: "We have never looked upon this fight as a regular stockholders fight. It was nothing more or less than an effort by a bunch of Wall Street pirates to take control of our company." Later, it was learned that some large blocks of shares had swung to Bell management in the last days of the fight because of Harvey Gaylord's efforts on Wall Street.

There was a party in the Frontier Room that day, but Larry had to excuse himself several times because his stomach was acting up. "Damn it, now I suppose they'll tell me I can't drink Pepto Bismol," Larry murmured as he headed for the door.

Larry finally excused himself and drove downtown for a haircut in the Liberty Bank building where his favorite barber worked. It gave him a chance to think about what he would say to the work force at a meeting scheduled for the production floor later in the day.

That afternoon, standing alone before the microphones, Larry wasn't especially impressive-looking: five-foot six, 170 pounds of businessman in a conservative businessman's suit; fidgety, chain-smoking, and stiff-faced because his ulcers were giving him pain. But his words were strong, and those who watched him looked at the light in the intense dark brown eyes under the black eyebrows.

"Now, today, we can go back to work and make up lost time," said Bell. "I wish to thank everyone who supported us in this fight, especially you loyal employes who stood back of me 100 percent."

It is ironic that less than a year later, controlling ownership of Bell passed into the hands of First York Corporation. Larry explained the matter in a letter to Reuben Fleet:

"They [First York] saw a good opportunity in Bell Aircraft, and as a result made a deal to take over the Martindell and associate holdings of Bell stock totaling some 70,000 shares. In addition they are asking for tenders for another 75,000 shares which they will probably get . . . a major portion thereof. The entire operation is friendly. We all like the crowd, and they seem to like us, and, of course, it eliminates the worry and threat of the Martindell group.

"Of course I am giving them no options on my stock and neither are any of our other staunch supporters and friendly stockholders.

"The whole transaction was brought about originally through Jack Bierwirth, one of our directors, and president of New York Trust Company. He is well acquainted with [David] Milton [of First York] and sits on the board of International Chemical with him. Mr. Milton and one of his associates will also join our board which will have a total of nine directors."

In July, 1960, the defense business of Bell Aircraft was sold to Textron Inc.

17

The Bell
Family Fight

To the rest of the world in 1948, Bell Aircraft was a wonder company, building the fastest airplanes in history. But inside the gates, emptiness and depression reigned. Fewer than two thousand insecure workers were left from the thirty thousand at the height of the war. Nearby was a vast army of laid-off workers who would line up at the gate at the slightest suspicion of a job opening and walk away in resentment and bitterness. What few jobs there were went to war veterans.

The days of *Bell News* and *Bellringer* were over. Union leaflets filled the need for something to read in the washrooms and cafeterias. Leadership of the UAW Local 501 was in the hands of the militant rank-and-filers. Some leaders were left wing and under investigation by the army-navy-air force personnel security board as possible subversives. Then, at a time when there was widespread fear of Communists, the *Buffalo Evening News* printed the names of several members of Local 501 who belonged to the "Socialist Workers' Party (Trotskyist)."

The Bell work force was stunned. Union elections brought new leaders, the Reutherites, into power. These men were solid unionists, loyal to Walter Reuther's international UAW and not at all interested in leftist ideology. They had one promise—that they could get more for the membership than the rank-and-filers could.

It wasn't a good time for getting much of anything from Bell Aircraft. In early 1949, Bell management had just written its third consecutive annual shareholder report explaining losses, not profits. The loss was $657,000 in 1946, $1.2 million in 1947, and $350,000 in 1948. Fat profits of the war years were over, but fat wages remained. Average hourly earnings at Bell in 1948 were $1.73, compared with the industry average of $1.57. Bell had been generous during its first fourteen years and now suffered for it. Contracts were scarce. Lean, low-paying companies were walking off with the work by underbidding Bell.

The beginning of major trouble with the local 501 had started in early 1948 when vice president of manufacturing Julius J. Domonkos—the tough, efficient administrator brought back from the Burlington Operations—put into effect a program aimed at making Bell more efficient.

"We've got a good chance to begin turning a profit again," Whitman told Domonkos at a meeting in the Frontier Room. The only other person present was Larry, sitting at the head of the table, who had been listening intently but not speaking.

"We'll make a profit when we get costs down." Bell injected.

"That's your job, Julius," Whitman told Domonkos. "We've got to reduce costs and get more competitive."

"You do your job, and we'll back you all the way," said Bell.

Except for the one-day walkout in 1945, there had never been serious labor trouble at Bell Aircraft. But when the hard line was instituted, the union was constantly in an uproar.

Domonkos announced that union officials must account for any time spent doing union business during working hours. "If the company pays a man's time, it't got a right to know what he's doing," said Domonkos.

Local 501's leaders responded bluntly: "You want to pipeline information to the foremen. Pretty soon you'll get no complaints, right?"

The union refused to fill out what they called Domonkos's "yellow dog forms," and several officials were not paid for unreported time. When the matter went to arbitration, the company won. The arbitrator said: "The union argues that it does a service in eliminating these [fancied grievances] without going to management. That is true. But if there are as many 'fancied grievances' as the time now spent would seem to indicate, the company is entitled to know about them in order, if possible, to eliminate the source of the grievance. . . . Such a person is a special problem and requires special treatment. If he is unjustly dealt with, he has the grievance procedure to protect him."

Round one went to managment and so did round two. Domonkos had his foremen keep track of the movements of union officials, and warnings were handed out to men found out of departments or in the cafeteria during working hours. One employee was given ten days suspension for absenteeism and tardiness.

The new leadership of Local 501 was elected on March 10, 1949, and sat down at the bargaining table with company representatives only four days before the April 30 expiration of the old contract. The challenge faced by Robert Siegler, president, and Mike Berdych, chairman, was a tough management backed up by sharp lawyers. And always in mind, the rough, radical ousted leftists waiting for an opportunity to get back into power.

Siegler and Berdych issued a leaflet that summed up the feelings of two men tossed into the water with sharks lurking below: "You realize there are some members of the local union who want us to fail in the hope that out of our failures they may rebuild their own political group. In fact, these individuals will try to make certain of our failure regardless of the cost to you or to the membership of the local union as a whole by attacking and undermining our support in the local union. They attack even now, hurling all sorts of accusations and slanders before we are installed in office—before our first meeting with the company. . . . We ask only a fair chance."

They had been elected on the basis of promises, and they were determined not to fall short. The union raised management eyebrows by laying on the table a set of demands that would have cost an estimated 62.5 cents per hour:

—A fifteen cent hourly wage increase.
—More than double the insurance program.
—A pension plan, when none existed elsewhere in the industry.
—Ten days sick leave, more holidays, triple time for holiday work, and a Christmas bonus of $10 for each year of seniority.

It was an initial bargaining position meant to open the way toward the lesser goals that the Local 501 bargaining committee had set for itself. But to management, the demands were deadly serious.

The contract was extended to May 15 and then to June 12,

while agreement was reached on some noneconomic matters. It was apparent that there would be no more deadline extensions. Domonkos and the management bargaining team showed up at the June bargaining session visibly fatigued from a late-hour session with Bell and Whitman. They put some important concessions on the table:

—A pension plan; union members would have to pay some of the cost, but it was a start.
—Higher minimum pay rates.
—More liberal provisions on vacation eligibility.

The membership rejected the company's offers. There was still time for more bargaining. Why rush? Management was bound to give in a little bit.

The vote to reject hurt Larry Bell deeply. "What're we supposed to do, lay down and let them tell us how to run this place?" he said to Whitman. "Not one more damn cent."

Two strike votes were held, and on June 10 it was agreed to bring in the Federal Mediation and Conciliation Service. Mediator Clarence LaMotte, after separate sessions with labor and management, told Larry: "You're still too far apart. There's no area for conciliation right now."

Across Niagara Falls Boulevard from the huge plant, a strike tent was erected. The first night Larry drove by it on his way to dinner, a group of employees stood sullenly at roadside while Bell waited for the light to change at the intersection. Larry fidgeted and whispered a curse, and as he drove away, he said, "That's the first time ever I haven't wanted to look into those faces."

Larry Bell gradually withdrew from direct participation in the dispute. The union announced it would strike on Monday, June 13, after a final meeting with the company. Regional UAW director Martin Gerber offered to put off demands for wages and pensions and extend the contract for four months and see the national pattern on wages and pensions for heavy industry. The offer was turned down.

"In view of the fact that Bell wages are already higher than the industry average," said Domonkos, "and in view of the fact that any further increases would seriously endanger Bell's competitive position, no increases in wages or vacation benefits can be granted. The pension plan is all we can offer at this time."

The strike began quietly in the early morning hours, like

friends showing up for a picnic. By mid-morning, nearly every-one in the seventeen hundred member local was at the plant gates. The kitchen tent was busy serving coffee, and traffic along the boulevard was slowed. But there was no violence. Management had shut the plant down to "avoid the possibility of picket line disturbances, violence, and injury to employes."

The two sides made some verbal exchanges, but as the days passed the number of pickets declined to one hundred fifty. A meeting with management was held June 30, at which the union declined to permit free access to nonstrikers.

"Enough of this," Whitman told Domonkos. "Let's set it up for an injunction."

On July 1, Bell photographers were flown in by helicopter to film an attempt by three carloads of engineers and supervisors to drive though the picket line. Word had leaked, and seven hundred pickets were ready and waiting to block the cars.

The next day, Domonkos went to a bargaining session with injunction papers in his pocket. The union lowered its wage increase demand by a nickel but held to its other demands. The company countered with a proposal that the strike be halted and that the talks on economic demands resume two weeks later.

"We're out, and we're going to stay out until you meet our demands," Siegler told management. As the meeting broke up, Domonkos handed Siegler the injunction papers. By court order, picketing was limited to "not more than fifteen pickets [at each entrance] . . . to be in motion and spaced in a single line" and "make way for trucks, automobiles, railroad cars, and any and all vehicles as well as persons on foot. . . ."

Public relations director Fran Dunn read the following message over the local radio stations: "All nonstriking employes of Bell Aircraft are requested to report for work at their regular starting time Wednesday. The plant is being opened following the granting of a Supreme Court injunction limiting picketing. The court ordered pickets to allow unmolested access to the plant."

The next morning, nearly one thousand engineers and non-strikers returned to work. Then the nonstriking three hundred member UAW Local 516 voted to return to work and crossed the picket line beginning July 25.

"There was no opposition from Local 501's pickets as the tool designers, timekeepers, production engineers and other

The sheriff's forces ready for a day's work during the Bell strike.

The picket line on Niagara Falls Blvd. outside the Bell plant in 1949.

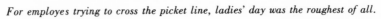

For employes trying to cross the picket line, ladies' day was the roughest of all.

Local 501 marches into the plant on August 19, 1949. Some nonstrikers caught on the job were attacked that day.

Larry, hospitalized by an auto accident in August 1949, is visited by Ray Whitman, left, and Julius Domonkos.

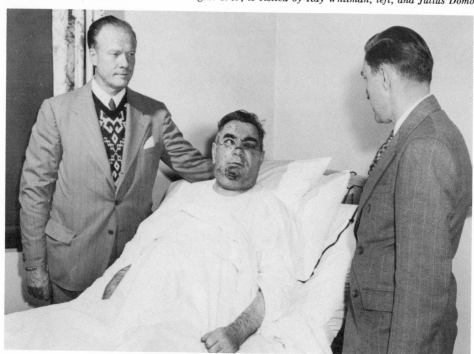

technicians who make up Local 516's membership passed through the gate," reported the *Courier-Express*.

The UAW had "no objection" to Local 516's action, "so long as they do not perform work normally performed by production and maintenance employes," said Edward F. Gray, UAW sub-regional director. The language was more direct on the picket line. The chant was "Scab!"

An intense union attack was directed at Domonkos. The union demanded that Domonkos be removed from his job. Larry, who had been silent since the strike began, responded: "My answer to this childish statement by Edward F. Gray is the same answer General Tony McAuliffe gave to Hitler—'Nuts.'"

Bell said the talks weren't deadlocked through Domonkos' fault but because the union refused to agree to a security clause "intended to keep members of subversive organizations, Communists, and Trotskyites from employment on or around restricted military projects in our plant."

Pressure on management began to mount because of the cost of the strike. Nearly thirteen hundred nonstrikers were reporting for work, but, except for some engineers doing design work, most had nothing to do. And for the union, there was the frustration of the stalled negotiations, fear that Domonkos was plotting to break Local 501, and then a startling announcement that Bell's production departments would reopen on August 11.

Domonkos claimed Bell was being made a "guinea pig" in a national UAW drive and, quoted the July 25 issue of *Aviation Week*, "United Auto Workers (CIO) Union is planning a major aircraft campaign. . . . The strike at Bell Aircraft Corp., says [UAW vice president John W.] Livingston, can properly be regarded as the start of the campaign."

Domonkos' letter to members of Local 501 invited them to come back to work: "Your job is ready for you—at the same wage rates, vacation plan, insurance coverage, and paid holidays that you had before the strike." There was this postscript: "It is requested that those who don't return to work arrange to take their tools and personal belongings out of the plant, since the company cannot be responsible for their loss."

The fight escalated. Piles of rocks began to show up at strategic places in the drainage ditches along the road. Steel helmets appeared on the heads of some pickets. The size of the strike posters diminished, but the sticks that held them got bigger.

Sheriff Henry Becker made arrangements for protecting non-strikers. Dave Forman, head of the Helicopter Division, prepared a helicopter for use by the deputies as a free "demonstrator," complete with pilot, siren, and Sheriff's Department markings.

On Friday, August 12, the scene at the gates was far worse than expected. A crowd of men and women, estimated at up to seven thousand five hundred, surrounded the plant. Local 501 was out in full force, and it was being joined by thousands of members of other western New York union locals.

Whitman was one of the first through the line. He was un-harmed, but several unionists put a shoulder to him in an at-tempt to knock him off his feet. The same happened to Domonkos. Other employes didn't fare so well. Some of the engineers entered the plant with bloody noses and torn shirts. Tires were slashed in the parking lots. Ripe tomatoes smacked the heads of some workers.

Sheriff Becker issued a call for volunteer deputies, and the company announced that, despite the violence, 1,028 employes were "at their jobs, including almost one hundred Local 501 members."

Siegler replied that "not a single one of the local's 1,700 strikers reported for work," and estimated that 30 members of Local 516 and 370 non-union employees entered the plant.

Vacation paychecks—withheld from strikers—greeted every unionist who went back to work. Those who did also received the following telegram from Siegler and Berdych: "Bell has never given you anything. UAW-CIO has won your high wages, seniority, insurance. Wall Street holding companies have now ordered Bell to smash your union. Stand firm now, and we will win. All CIO is backing you. Don't scab. Stick to your union. Victory is near."

Some unionists were visited at their homes by Local 501 "flying squads." Holdouts were the subject of neighborhood disgrace when strikers distributed leaflets nearby that called them scabs.

The strike was ever-changing. One day there would be a demonstration of men in uniform carrying American flags, the next day a solid line of women pushing baby carriages. (One carriage had a sign "Scab Children Can't Play With Me.") Helicopters carrying executives and supplies in and out of the plant would buzz low over the heads of the pickets, blowing dust and debris over them. The pickets protected themselves by sending up large helium-filled balloons on hundred-foot strings. Deputies and nonstrikers shot the balloons down. The sheriff brought in horses for crowd control, so the pickets shot air rifles at the horses. The neighboring county of Orleans sent forty deputies to help out, and arrests were made for violations of the court injunction against mass picketing.

Then, at 9:30 A.M. August 19, Local 501 used what it called the "new weapon of labor." About five hundred pickets staged a fake return to work, walking shoulder to shoulder through a company gate displaying employe badges for the plant guards to see. They marched like an army around the huge production floor.

"What the hell are you doing?" Whitman shouted to Siegler.

"It's a back-to-work movement," shouted Siegler, "and these back-to-work movements sometimes get out of hand."

The strikers stayed in the plant for half an hour. Men at work were terrorized and ran for cover. There wasn't a toilet in the plant that wasn't in use with the door locked. Other workers headed for the back doors, but several men were caught and beaten. A few were forcibly carried out of the plant.

Larry Bell and Sheriff Becker wired Governor Dewey asking for state help in restoring peace. The governor responded by stating that Becker "has complete and unlimited power to deputize any number" of deputies and that "as governor, I expect you to discharge your responsibilities." Dewey wanted no part of the mess.

The leaders of Local 516 announced: "We, the membership of Local 516 Bell units, do not approve of the action taken by the UAW-CIO and Local 501 this nineteenth day of August. The unauthorized entry into this plant for the purpose of committing bodily harm upon persons employed in this factory, some of whom were 516 members. It is deplorable that during this day and age such conditions exist. We appeal to the executive board of the international union and ask that they do all in their power to prevent repetition of this display of un-Americanism again."

Leonard G. Feldmann, business editor at the *Courier-Express*, wrote that "if the Messrs. Bell and Reuther would sit down together at a table, it would put an end to mob violence at the Bell plant. We feel sure this area would welcome Reuther. . . ."

Reuther kept his distance, and the violence continued. Masked men beat up a group of workers headed across the Niagara Falls airport taxi strips toward the plant. In an aircraft control tower atop the administration building, deputies used high-powered binoculars to keep track of the movements of crowds of pickets—radioing information to company buses carrying workers so they could attempt to enter at a gate with the smallest crowd. When buses were rocked and the windows broken, the company installed wire mesh over new windows and knife blades were bolted to the bottom edges of the vehicles. Union men blew tires by spreading hundreds of carpet tacks at the plant entrance.

There were a few light moments in the day-to-day struggle. One came when a pair of Niagara Falls honeymooners absentmindedly joined a caravan of plant-bound Bell workers. As the line of cars neared Gate 1, crowds of jeering pickets gave the honeymooners no alternative than to stay with the caravan into the plant. They frantically drove around the grounds looking for a way out, then flagged a Bell security guard for help.

But the battlers saw no humor. Local 501 sent a leaflet to the nonunion employees that stated: "Those foremen, and we know who they are, who have been calling up our members and making them tempting little offers to induce them to betray their union and fellowmen, are going to be remembered. Local 501 appeals to those of you who have a shred of decency to stand up and be counted with the trade unionists, not the strike breakers."

September 7 was an especially rough day. The strikers and their friends showed up in force. There were at least two hundred pickets at Gate 1 that marched three abreast in lockstep formation. Sixteen workers were injured, including Marge Banhalzl of the accounting department, who was clubbed on the legs while trying to get into the plant. Just to the north, employees were beaten in a widespread running battle that extended from a street corner, over fields, and into nearby homes, where pursued workers ran for safety.

District attorney William Miller came to the scene for the first time to direct arrests. He spoke at a workers' rally in the plant and at the end of the day phoned the governor to request again that the state militia be brought to the scene.

In late August, Larry crashed his car on the way home from work and spent most of the rest of the strike in the hospital.

Larry's head hit the windshield, his jaw was broken and his face badly scarred, but his life was not endangered.

On September 13, the company and union resumed meetings and incidents on the picket line subsided. But when the talks once again broke down, a major conflict took place. A convoy of five company buses and autos containing 307 workers tried to break. As the vehicles approached, deputies formed a line on each side of the road to block a rush by the strikers. Stones were tossed, and several deputies were hit before tear gas was fired. Nearly ten deputies were injured by rocks.

Each confrontation became more intense, and it was rumored that a full scale plant invasion was set for Thursday, October 6. "Bigger than August 19," a picket shouted.

Larry wired President Truman and Air Secretary Symington when he learned that telegrams had been sent by union officials requesting a halt to federal expenditures at Bell. The same night, October 5, a delegation of four air force officers arrived to supervise the protection of classified documents and government property in the event of a striker invasion. Military troops in the New York City area were alerted to be flown to Niagara Falls, if needed.

On the morning of October 6, instead of an invasion, several ministers and former divinity students held a prayer service for the strikers across from Gate 1. The war of nerves seemed to have no end. But that same day, the state industrial commissioner, Edward Corsi, announced the appointment of a board of inquiry headed by the chancellor of Cornell University. It was apparent that someone high in federal government, possibly President Truman, had taken action. Hearings and conferences continued Saturday, October 15, all through Sunday, and into the morning hours of Monday before an agreement was reached that ended the strike:

"The company and the Union hereby mutually agree to submit to the Board of Inquiry for arbitration all matters which either party has considered an issue in dispute during the period of the 1949 contract negotiations. The decision of the Board with respect to any and all such matters shall be final. . . .

"With respect to men who have returned to work during the strike, it is agreed that seniority and other rights as employees shall be preserved and that the Union will not take disciplinary measures against such men, nor will they be required to join the

Union. Pending arbitration findings by the board, the company and the Union will continue to abide by the provisions of the contract which expired, as extended, on June 12, 1949."

Ray Whitman said later, "Management reversed its previous position [against] arbitration largely because of the known quality of the arbitration panel and because the corporation would have been under tremendous pressure to accept the board's findings even if they were not mandatory while the union would not be nearly so susceptible to similar pressure."

There was also political pressure. Congressman Anthony J. Tauriello had announced he was opposed to the company stand and was attempting to get the air force to intervene in the strike. Then, on October 4, the Buffalo Common Council had voted that it "publicly condemns the Bell Aircraft Corporation for the methods it has employed during this controversy and demands forthwith that the differences between labor and management be resolved so that the hardship which has ensued from this strike may be ended and that the strikebound workers be restored to their jobs."

In a Sunday column, editor Feldmann had put it more directly: "Frankly, we think the public is getting fed up with the entire affair."

The arbitration award made on January 10, 1950, was a bitter disappointment to the union:

—No mention of the pension plan offered by the company before the strike began.

—Pay increase of 5 cents per hour, but 2.5 cents of this would be used as an employee contribution to an expanded insurance program.

—A new government security clause aimed at keeping subversives out of the plant.

—Employes hired during the strike could stay on the job without joining the union.

—An agreement reached earlier between the management and Local 501 that employees with five years or more seniority get two days additional vacation per year was not mentioned in the arbitration award.

An opinion was scrawled in a washroom near the production floor: "Sold down the river."

18

Highest

and Fastest

Fifty years after the Wright brothers' first powered flight, Larry Bell's airplanes were setting altitude and speed records of more than 70,000 feet and more than 1,600 miles per hour. Major Chuck Yeager had flown faster than 1,600 mph over Edwards Air Force Base on December 12, 1953—flying the X-1A, an improved version of the X-1. The X-1A was nearly five feet longer, had increased tank space, and was equipped with a turbine pump to force feed rocket propellants. The pump, which Bell had wanted to use in the X-1 but was not available in time, replaced the earlier nitrogen pressure system.

Because of its built-in limitations, the original X-1 was flown no faster than 967 mph at an altitude of 70,140 feet. But other advanced aircraft were being developed, from World War II through the early 1950s. It was an exciting time for the engineers whose designs were making Bell the leader in the most advanced areas of experimental flight.

Bell Aircraft built ten airplanes in the X-series and provided the reaction-control thrusters for the North American X-15. Through the early 1950s, a constant turmoil of ideas, briefings, flights, debriefings, modifications, and redesigning took place. It was the beginning of the push to put man in space, although no one realized that would be the outcome.

Even Larry remained conservative, at least in public. "We will conceive and build vehicles with speed ranges of between Mach 10 and Mach 20 [approximately 7,000 and 14,000 mph] and the ability to operate at altitudes up to fifty miles," he said at the time. "And this we will do in the next two decades."

223

Larry takes a look at the X-1A.

Larry greets Chuck Yeager after an X-1A test.

Man was walking on the moon within fifteen years.

There was more to the Bell effort than speed and altitude. Bob Woods had brought out of Germany in 1945 an unfinished experimental aircraft, the Messerschmitt P-1101, that contained the crude beginnings of a pivoting wing. Aeronautical engineers had long before come to the conclusion that a delta, or sweep-wing, would be ideal for high-speed flight. The problem was that a swept-back wing performed poorly and was dangerous at low speed. A variable-sweep wing, if it could be made simple, workable, and practical, would be a great benefit to the future of aviation.

American troops had arrived at the Messerschmitt plant before the P-1101 was finished. Its wings were adjustable only on the ground. It had no mechanism to compensate for the shifting center-of-lift, but it was ideal for swing-wing experiments. The wheels, fuel, and jet engine were all contained in the fuselage. Nothing interfered with the wings.

Woods nearly completed the P-1101 at the Messerschmitt plant in Oberammergau, working with some of the German designers he had found in nearby communities. But they were hampered by the fact that drawings and background data had been stored, for safekeeping, elsewhere. French forces had found these papers, and the papers had disappeared.

The airplane was shipped to Wright Field, but later it was shipped to the Niagara Falls plant for examination and development. Bob Woods designed a system that solved the shifting center-of-lift problem. This was achieved by having the wings move along the fuselage as the sweep angle varied. Thus the Bell X-5 was born. Two fat-bellied research aircraft that closely resembled the P-1101 were built at the Niagara Falls plant. The first flight of an X-5 was on June 20, 1951; first flight with variable sweep was made July 27. It worked. The X-5 flight test program was to succeed in proving the concept of the variable-sweep wing.

The P-1101 had been dismembered in the process of building the X-5s. Nothing but scrap was left of it when the other planes were rolled off the production floor. But the story of this German airplane was a favorite of Larry Bell. "Messerschmitt was determined to preserve the P-1101 as the war came to an end," he recalled. "They took it down the road one night and hid it in a mountain cave, but Bob Woods found it anyway."

Bell loved to tell of such exploits. His voice had become

gravelly. There was also a hint of a speech impediment caused by the car crash injuries that hospitalized him in 1949.

Trips to the hospital were put to good use. The 1949 experience trapped him in bed with his broken jaw wired shut. It forced him to be idle, or at least stationary (he ran the company by murmuring instructions over the phone). Later, when he was hospitalized with mumps, he gave TV sets to the area's convalescent hospitals and homes for the aged. "A wonderful companion for shut-ins," said Bell. At that time, there weren't many TV sets anywhere, and hardly any of the institutions that received a set from Bell had owned one before.

Larry had a lifetime affection for disabled persons, for children, and for pet dogs. At one time in the 1930s, he owned four dogs, and in 1937, the Bell home in Eggertsville was the romping ground for animals named Belarus, Duncan, and Hunter. For the convenience of the pets he brought to work, an artificial fire hydrant was installed on the flat roof over Larry's office.

When Madame Henri Bonnet, wife of the French ambassador, called Larry in 1950 to ask if he might be able to help a woman whose face had been totally disfigured, Larry remembered his crippled boyhood friend, Morrison Rockhill. The answer was an immediate yes.

American plastic surgeons were doing wonders for Madame Jacqueline Auriol, the famous French flier who had been disfigured in a 1949 crash. A team of doctors headed by Dr. John Marquis Converse, of the Manhattan Eye, Ear, and Throat Hospital in New York City, was rebuilding the face of the daughter-in-law of French President Vincent Auriol. Face-building was a tedious, delicate process. As the effort neared the twenty-second and final operation, Jacqueline became despondent and developed a fear that she might never fly again.

Through Mme. Bonnet, Mme. Auriol had met Larry Bell, and through Larry, the Bell helicopter. Flying lessons were arranged at the Niagara Falls plant, and within four weeks Jacqueline was an accomplished helicopter pilot. A lasting affection between Larry and Jacqueline had developed, as well, but the young woman was disturbed by the publicity she thought Larry was planning. Plant movie photographers were constantly filming her activities. When she asked why, she was told it was Mr. Bell's personal order. Jacqueline was irritated, but since Larry was providing a helicopter and instruction without charge, she ignored the matter.

On her last night in Buffalo, in early 1951, Larry held a dinner party in Jacqueline's honor. When it was over, Larry leaned close to Mme. Auriol and whispered: "Dear Jacqueline, the first time I met you, you told me you were dreadfully worried at the thought of seeing your children again with your new face. Don't worry any more about it. They have already seen it. That cameraman who so annoyed you made only one copy of his film—the one I sent to your husband. Your children have seen it. Set your heart at rest; go home. They're waiting for you."*

There was no fear or surprise in the faces of her two young sons when the family met her at Orly Airport, although it was not the face of the mother they had known from before the plane crash. The doctors had performed a marvel in rebuilding a face similar to Jacqueline's original beautiful face. The accident had left only her eyes intact; the break-up of her facial bones had brought about a collapse of the muscles of her face, causing it to sag to her neck and around her disfigured mouth and broken nose. Without plastic surgery, Jacqueline would not have been able to lead a normal life.

Some time later, she wrote to Bell: ". . . I have the impression that all is new for me! My friends, my home, my life. Oh Larry, hurrah, bravo for the Freedom! I kiss you."

As a result of his experience with Mme. Auriol, Larry helped establish a clinic for reconstructive plastic surgery at Dr. Converse's hospital. Larry's Society for the Rehabilitation of the Facially Disfigured provided funds for this clinic, which opened in 1955 and was equipped to treat facial disfigurement, as well as the psycho-social and vocational problems associated with the facially disfigured.

The most spectacular of Bell Aircraft's experimental planes was the X-2, a swept-wing rocket-powered vehicle that took man faster and higher than ever before. The X-2 achieved a 2,148-mph record on September 27, 1956, in a flight that took the life of its pilot, Air Force Captain Milburn G. Apt. An earlier flight that year by Captain Iven Kincheloe set an altitude record of 126,200 feet—twenty-four miles into space.

---

*From *I Live to Fly* by Jacqueline Auriol, translated by Pamela Swinglehurst. Copyright © 1968 by Opera Mundi; English translation © 1970 by E. P. Dutton and Michael Joseph Ltd. Reprinted by permission of the publishers, E. P. Dutton.

The X-2 was conceived in 1945 by the air force, NACA, and Bell as the successor to the X-1. The goal was to build an airplane capable of exploring the effects of flight at speeds and altitudes not possible with the X-1. Findings were for use by the entire aviation industry.

Stanley W. Smith was named project engineer for Bell. Others who participated in the design beginnings of the X-2 were Paul Emmons, Jack Strickler, Jack Woolams, Bob Stanley, Charles Fay, and Harold Hawkens. They produced an airplane with stainless steel wings sharply swept back 40 degrees. It was powered by a Curtiss-Wright rocket engine that could be throttled to 15,000 pounds of thrust, two and a half times the power of the X-1. The cockpit was surrounded by glass wool to protect it from outside temperatures of nearly 1,000 degrees, caused by air friction at high speed. The entire pressurized cabin could be jettisoned by explosive charges so the pilot could ride it to a lower altitude for bailout in case of emergency.

Plane number two (46-675) was completed first in the two-aircraft building program. The engine wasn't ready when roll-out took place on November 11, 1950, so ground trials were conducted with the B-50 "mother" aircraft that would carry the X-2 aloft for its rocket flights.

The first unpowered glide test did not take place until June 27, 1952, over Edwards Air Force Base, California. Bell test pilot Jean "Skip" Ziegler was at the controls, and, except for some landing gear problems, the test went flawlessly.

The engine still wasn't ready nearly a year later, but it was decided the time had come for tests of the fuel system and some engine components. The X-2 was powered by liquid oxygen and a mix of ethyl alcohol and water.

On May 12, 1953, Ziegler climbed into the X-2 cockpit and was carried aloft for a routine flight in which the X-2 was to remain in the bomb bay of the B-50. It ended in disaster, far out over Lake Ontario. The research plane exploded, and what was left of it was immediately jettisoned into the lake. Ziegler was killed instantly, and a crewman, Frank Walko, was blown out of the bomb bay by the explosion. Neither body was ever found. Bell pilot William Leyshon showed great skill in bringing the crippled bomber back to the Niagara Falls airport for a safe landing.

It was a year before an accident investigation board was able

to find the cause of the explosion. It was discovered that standard leather gaskets tended to absorb rocket fuels and, under
momentary stress, would explode, setting off a chain-reaction
fuel explosion. A different type of gasket was substituted, and
the problem was solved.

The combination of tragedy and daring exploits that accompanied the Bell X-series drew a great amount of public attention. An X-2 film, "Toward the Unknown," starring William
Holden, was made by Warner Brothers in the mid-1950s. By
the time it premiered in Buffalo, public relations director Fran
Dunn and Holden had become friends, having spent many hours
together on the road promoting the film. The two visited Larry at
his apartment before the reception, since Bell was sick and
under doctor's orders to stay in bed.

Walking the short distance up Delaware Avenue to the Saturn
Club, Dunn asked Holden for a small favor.

"Name it," said Holden.

"My wife," said Dunn, "will be standing just inside the door
waiting for me. The rest of the Bell executives, and their wives,
will be gathered a little further inside. Would you give Mrs.
Dunn a warm greeting, as though you knew her?"

When they walked in, Holden practically swept Mrs. Dunn
off her feet. The crowd went silent, Mrs. Dunn nearly fainted,
and Fran innocently looked the other way.

"Oh, my God," Mrs. Dunn whispered to her husband as
Holden moved on to meet his hosts.

Beginning with Larry's brother Grover's crash in 1913, death
had haunted Bell's aviation career. Except for helicopters, he
had a personal fear of the brutal, violent death that high speed
could deliver to the men and women who chose to fly. Late in
his life, he spoke of guided missiles as an inevitable successor
to manned aircraft. "You don't have to ask any mother's son to
ride a missile," he said. He named the Rascal missile "Pilot
Saver." It was a typical Larry Bell phrase, combining his con-
victions with his flair for salesmanship. The head of the company that built the world's fastest and highest-flying airplanes
didn't believe in the future of manned combat flight. A basic
Bell concept was this: "We've spent the lives of many of our
best young men to get this far in aviation. Now let's let man-
made instruments and electronics do the risky flying."

One death that caused special sorrow was that of Jack
Woolams, Bell's brilliant chief test pilot. It was intended that

Larry and Jacqueline Auriol in 1951, when she learned to fly the helicopter and Larry fell in love.

Capt. Ivan Kincheloe (pressure suit) after his record-breaking high altitude flight of 126,200 feet in the X-2.

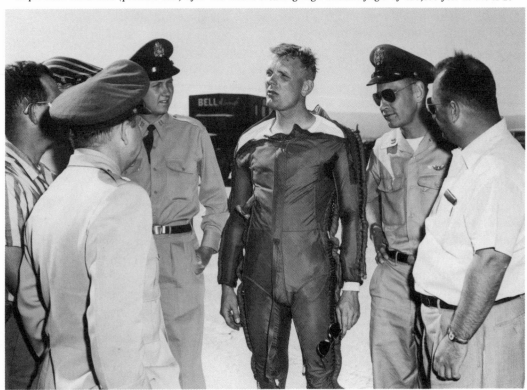

X-1 No. 3, which exploded and burned on the ground, November 9, 1951. Pilot Joe Cannon was hospitalized with burns.

Lt. Col. Frank Everest in the cockpit of the X-2.

X-5 in flight, wings swept back.

Bell test pilot Jean L. "Skip" Ziegler and Roy Sandstrom, vice president of engineering with the X-2 in which Ziegler died on May 12, 1953.

Larry confers with Gen. Oliver P. Echols.

Jack Woolams is congratulated by Bob Woods and Larry Bell following the first XP-77 test flight on April 1, 1944.

RECONNAISSANCE AIRPLANE

X-16

USAF

Artist's concept of the X-16 "Bald Eagle."

The remains of Mel Apt's X-2.

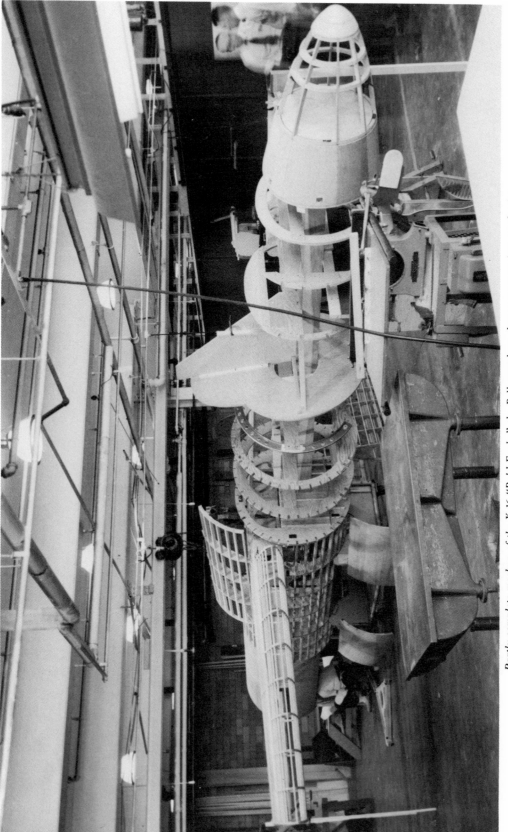

Partly-complete mockup of the X-16 "Bald Eagle," the Bell spy plane that never went into production.

Larry gets a TP-39 ride. On the wing is Peter Running of Flight Operations. It was rumored, but never confirmed, that Bob Stanley put the aircraft through some extreme maneuvers on this flight and that Larry became violently airsick.

The Bell L-39-1 (a P-63 with an experimental wing), first American swept-wing airplane.

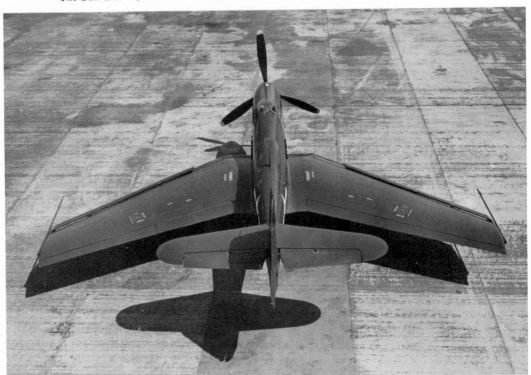

Courtesy William G. Johnston

The XS-1 and the Spirit of St. Louis in the main hall of the Smithsonian Institution's Air and Space Museum.

A space shuttle concept thirty years ahead of its time. These artist's drawings show what Walter Dornberger had in mind in suggesting that Larry develop an airplane that could shuttle back and forth from space. In the launch concept, note the hot gas exhaust system at far left.

Woolams be the first man to attempt to break the sound barrier in the X-1, but he died when his souped-up P-39, Cobra I, crashed into Lake Ontario on August 30, 1946. The next day, Tex Johnston won the National Air Race at Cleveland, flying Cobra II against the best fighters in the world. The race proved a point that was important to Bell Aircraft: nothing could match the P-39 at low altitude. But the effort had cost Larry a dear friend.

There was near-tragedy in the X-series program when test pilot Joe Cannon was burned by an explosion and fire aboard X-1 No. 3, named Queenie. The aircraft was destroyed before its first flight, but Cannon recovered. Craft number two in the series was test flown by NACA and later modified to include a turbo-pump fuel system and other changes. It was redesignated as X-1E.

Chuck Yeager received the International Harmon Trophy for flying the X-1A at 1,650 mph. Later, Colonel Frank K. Everest won the same trophy for flying the X-2 at 1,900 mph. The altitude record of 126,200 feet was set by Captain Iven Kincheloe, who received the McKay Trophy for his accomplishment. Another of the key test pilots was Major Arthur "Kit" Murray, who set a record of 90,000 feet in the X-1A.

Three improved versions followed the original three X-1s. Aircraft X-1A, -1B and -1D were five feet longer, had an extra five feet of wing span, and weighed a thousand pounds more than the earlier experimental aircraft. All were powered by the 6,000-pound thrust rocket engine built by Reaction Motors Inc. Extra fuel carried in the larger aircraft gave the engine a longer burning time and the potential to fly higher and faster.

In a secret, unrelated effort at this time, the Bell X-16 "Bald Eagle" was in development for the air force as a twin-engine jet capable of performing photographic missions high over the continent of Russia. But no X-16 was ever built. The company was still in negotiation for production of twenty-two aircraft when the air force suddenly canceled the entire top-secret program.

Lockheed had beaten Bell by building and flying the U-2, a single-engine spy plane designed for the same task. Bell had won out over proposals submitted by Fairchild and Martin and was ahead of schedule when Lockheed's entry became known.

The State Department later denied any involvement in the U-2 program before Lockheed had test flown the aircraft. However, in 1976, the Senate Intelligence Committee quoted former CIA chief William Colby as saying: "The development of the U-2 aircraft as an effective collection device would not have been possible if the CIA budget had been a matter of public knowledge. Our budget increased significantly during the development phase of that aircraft. That fact, if public, would have attracted attention."

There is the possibility that the air force and the CIA were funding spy plane programs separately and in such great secrecy that one organization did not know what the other was doing until the first U-2 flight became known. Whatever the reason, Bell contract representatives said they had never seen a program dropped so unexpectedly. "The curtain came down while I was in flight to Dayton for negotiation on the production order," said John J. Weisbeck, Jr. "Everything was going smoothly when I left Buffalo. When I landed, I checked with the Bell office in Dayton by phone from the airport. Charley Hall told me, 'There is no more X-16 program. We just got word. You might as well go home.'"

The days of fixed-wing aircraft production programs at Bell Aircraft were coming to an end. As he had in the past, Larry was out in the shop to talk to the workers and boost morale when the X-16 project folded. No one in the company knew when he might see Larry Bell, who constantly moved through the offices and the plant. Once, in the early 1950s, Larry walked up to a worker, introduced himself, and handed the man a pair of rosaries blessed by Pope Pius XII. "These are for you and your wife," said Bell. "Thanks for praying for me in 1949." The man had stopped at the hospital after Larry's auto accident and had told him his Catholic family was praying for a speedy recovery. Larry remembered this and took rosaries with him to an audience with the Pope when he visited Italy.

Bell Aircraft would provide reaction control thrust chambers for the North American X-15, the research airplane that succeeded the X-2, but there was a spectacular and tragic finish in store before the Bell X-series passed into history. On September 27, 1956, Captain Milburn G. Apt became the first man to reach Mach 3—2,148 mph—in a flight over Edwards Air Force Base that took his life.

Apt was an experienced test pilot but had never flown the X-2. Everything went smoothly through the complete engine burn. At 72,000 feet, Apt nosed over the X-2 and dived to

66,000 feet, where the aircraft reached a record top speed of Mach 3.196. Seconds later he lost control, his aircraft spinning through the sky and tossing him about in the cockpit. At 40,000 feet, Apt pulled the handle to eject the cabin and then at a low altitude, he jettisoned the canopy and released his seat belt. But there apparently was no time left. Captain Apt was still in the seat when the cabin hit the dry lake bed at more than 100 mph. He was killed instantly. There was never an explanation for why he lost control of the structurally sound airplane.

Here's what became of the Bell X-series airplanes:

XS-1 —On exhibit in the main hall of the Smithsonian Institution's Air and Space Museum, Washington, D. C. Named "Glamorous Glennis."

X-1 No. 2—Modified and redesignated X-1E. Now mounted on a pedestal in the NASA Flight Research Center, Edwards Air Force Base, California. Named "Little Joe."

X-1 No. 3—Exploded and burned during ground tests at the east end of the South Base ramp at Edwards Air Force Base on November 9, 1951. Joe Cannon, Bell test pilot, was hospitalized. Aircraft named "Queenie."

X-1A —Exploded on a NACA captive flight on August 8, 1955, and was jettisoned. The aircraft fell to the bombing range at Edwards AFB.

X-1B —Transferred to the Air Force Museum, Wright-Patterson Air Force Base, Dayton, Ohio, in 1958 after completing its final research flight in 1957.

X-1D —Destroyed on its first captive flight, August 23, 1951, over Edwards Air Force Base.

X-2 No. 1—Exploded while still captive over Lake Ontario. Pilot Jean L. (Skip) Ziegler and B-50 crewman Frank Walko were killed.

X-2 No. 2—Went out of control and was destroyed on September 27, 1956, after Captain Milburn G. Apt had flown it to Mach 3—2,148 mph over Edwards Air Force Base. Captain Apt ejected but was killed.

X-5 No. 1—Now at the U.S. Air Force Museum at Wright-Patterson Air Force Base.

X-5 No. 2—Crashed at Edwards Air Force Base on October 14, 1953, during spin tests. Pilot Major Raymond A. Popson was killed.

19

Back to

Mentone

It was a warm Sunday morning so still the dew fell like rain-drops from the leaves of the giant elms along Delaware Avenue. A slow toll droned solemnly down from St. Joseph's New Cathedral as Larry stood slouched at the window, watching pedestrians and the casual traffic below. "Irma," he said quietly to his housekeeper, "let's take the car out."

They drove aimlessly, moving slowly down some of the streets where Bell Aircraft executives owned large houses and were raising families. Then Larry headed northwest in the direction of the plant. Irma Brooks knew what to expect.

"Are you going to make me walk around in that place again?"

"You can stay in my office," he said.

As they walked toward the administration building through the executive parking lot, Larry gestured at the empty parking places. "All these vice presidents worry about big problems," Bell murmured. "Details become big problems. If I had enough people who watched details, I wouldn't need vice presidents."

Late that afternoon, Larry chuckled when he walked back into his office and found Irma on the couch, sleeping. "Let's get something to eat," he said, awakening her.

Over dinner, he described plans to hold a banquet honoring the employees who started the Elmwood Avenue plant in 1935. "I'll get Fran Dunn working on it in the morning," he said. "What a treat it would be to get together with Jimmy Smith, Andrew Grojean, and the others."

That night, Larry suffered severe chest pains and cried out

for help. Irma frantically dialed Dr. Eugene J. Lippschutz, the heart specialist who had been treating Bell for some time. Larry recovered in the hospital, but decided to follow the doctor's advice and reduce his work load. After a meeting of the directors, it was announced on October 2, 1954 that Larry had resigned from his position as general manager. Leston P. Faneuf was elected to succeed him and William G. Gisel, comptroller, was named to additional duties as secretary. Larry continued to hold the title of president.

To help smooth the transition for the new management team, Larry scheduled a trip to Wichita, Kansas, where Boeing had a major plant. Bell Aircraft was building jet engine nacelles for the B-47 and B-52 bombers under Boeing subcontracts. Good customer relations required an occasional visit by the company president.

Larry was met at the railroad station by resident Bell representative Ed Paskus, who drove a tattered brown Hudson wearing a white mantle of bird droppings. Two smears on the front window indicated an attempt at driver visibility.

Empty bottles and cans rattled under the seat, and the car smelled of stale laundry and poolrooms. "Larry," said Paskus as they drove away, "it might be a good idea for the company to supply a new car here. I'm driving all the time." There was no reply, so Paskus continued to describe his transportation problems all the way to the hotel. Larry kept silent, but just as the car stopped, he slapped a hand on the dashboard and said, "By God, they don't make cars like this anymore!"

The bomber subassembly program was going well. Boeing expressed satisfaction with Bell's costs, quality, and delivery, and Larry left town pleased. Feeling in high spirits, he phoned his office to have travel arrangements made for him to visit his friends in France—Mme. Auriol and her family.

When he returned to Buffalo, Larry learned that there would be a two-week delay before his ship left from New York, so he went back to a work schedule at the plant. Larry kept his hours to a minimum, but at night, there was a constant flow of dinner visitors to his apartment.

Conversations almost always turned to some event in aviation history from which Larry had collected a memento. Bell never threw anything away. He had newspaper clippings dating from the Wright brothers flight in 1903, ticket stubs from the 1910 aviation meet in California, and airplane parts, medals, models, and photographs. All these things were carefully wrapped and stored in a spare room. Two of Larry's most cherished relics were his brother's leather flying helmet and the steering wheel from the plane in which Grover had crashed.

Frequently, late at night, Irma Brooks would be summoned to bring objects out of the storeroom, then wrap them again when Larry and his guests had looked at them. "You ought to have a museum," she said one night. He paid no attention, so Irma took things into her own hands.

When Larry left for Europe, she made arrangements to have the spare room set up to display the Bell mementos. Each item was carefully cleaned and mounted and placed in glass cases or on the walls around the room. Suitable lighting was installed.

By the time Bell returned, the job was complete. Weary from the trip, Larry sat down heavily and took a sip of scotch and soda. "God, I'm glad to be back," he said.

"Mr. Bell, I have a surprise for you," said Irma, smiling nervously.

"Is it going to cost a lot of money?"

"Oh, you know everything costs you a lot. Come and see it."

When they walked into the next room, Irma turned on the lights. Larry looked around in astonishment, then sat down on a chair in the middle of the room. "It's my life," he said with a voice full of emotion. "It's my whole life."

Larry returned to work vigorously. There were endless details to be handled. The company had grown to encompass five wholly owned subsidiaries: the Wheelabrator Corporation, Mishawaka, Indiana; the W. J. Schoenberger Company, Cleveland, Ohio; the Hydraulic Research and Manufacturing Company, Burbank, California; the Bell Automation Corporation, Rochester, New York, and the Bell Exploration and Development Corporation, Fort Worth, Texas.

The company reported $185.6 million in sales for 1954. Employment was 18,850 and continuing to rise. Helicopter sales from the Texas plant were increasing, and engineering innovations continued to pour out of Bell facilities.

The first jet-powered vertical take-off and landing (VTOL) airplane was flown by test pilot Davy Howe on November 16, 1954. This one-ton test airplane was powered by two thousand-pound jet engines that rotated from vertical for takeoff to horizontal for forward flight. The company-funded Bell VTOL featured a solution to the problem of controlling aircraft in low

Larry spends a quiet moment in his museum.

One of Larry's last formal portraits.

speed and hovering flight. Air from a compressor was ducted to the tail and the wing tips. During hover, when there wasn't forward speed to make the regular control surfaces useful, the pilot maneuvered by directing this compressor thrust.

The U.S. Army funded another VTOL, the XV-3 converti-plane, first flown in 1955. This aircraft had three-bladed pro-pellers at each end of its wings. For forward flight, the units tilted 90 degrees forward and served as propellers. For hover-ing, they moved to a horizontal position and provided helicopter-style lift.

But aircraft, even helicopters, were only a Bell sideline in 1955. In his annual report message for that year Larry said: "More than 75 percent of our scientific and technical effort in 1955 was concerned with guided missiles and related work. Our greatest single effort was expended on the air force GAM-63 Rascal missile which has already been identified as an air-to-surface missile of advanced design."

The message also hinted of farewell: "To the directors and officers, and to all the executives and employees of the com-pany and its subsidiaries, I would like to express thanks for their hard work and loyal efforts."

The company's wide range of capabilities resulted in an air force contract to produce the complete missile named Rascal. In a massive, pioneering effort, Bell was responsible for the original design and development, fabrication of the airframe, guidance system, rocket engines, ground support equipment, launching equipment, and training aids, as well as the flight-testing program. It was one of the biggest and most diverse single programs ever undertaken by Bell Aircraft. The Rascal program produced pioneer work in missile development and production that became standards of the industry.

Another development project that became a production item in 1955 was the U.S. Navy's Automatic Carrier Landing Sys-tem, ACLS, which Bell had been working on for four years. Flight tests of a feasibility model were conducted in 1953, and the first fully automatic landing—in which the pilot did not touch the controls—was made by a navy F-3D fighter at the Niagara Falls airport on May 5, 1954.

The ACLS used computers and radars aboard the ship to solve the biggest problem faced by navy pilots—how to land safely aboard a moving, swaying carrier deck at exactly the right speed and at the right spot to engage the aircraft's

XV-3 in forward flight. For vertical takeoff, its giant propellers shifted to the horizontal position.

The Bell VTOL lifting off. For forward flight, its two barrel-shaped engines turned to produce rearward jet thrust.

tailhook. The problem is intensified by night flying and rough weather.

Bell's equipment compensated for the pitch, roll, heave, and yaw of the ship and sent the proper signals to the aircraft's automatic pilot for a safe landing. The pilot had the option to take control at any time. It was a success, popular with the pilots, and was destined to be installed in all the large U.S. Navy carriers.

In the later years of his life, Larry frequently spoke of his boyhood in Mentone. He had returned several times through the years when a short side-trip could be arranged from Chicago or Detroit, and his life-long friend Morrison Rockhill frequently brought home-town news to Buffalo.

Larry joked about the size of Mentone, saying it had a population of 450, "when everybody's home." When the community held a "Larry Bell Day" during the 1941 summer fair, he and Lucille arranged to be there. At that time, Larry had more than eleven thousand employes working on a backlog of business ranging near $100 million. But there was time for a trip to see the people in the town where he was born. As they passed Warsaw on the last leg of the trip, the Bells were delighted to see the telephone poles along the road were posted with signs reading: "Welcome home, Lawrence Bell."

Several events were scheduled in his honor, beginning with a reception held in the local drugstore because there was no hall. A school band of boys and girls led a march through town to the fairgrounds, with Larry and Lucille leading the parade, accompanied by town officials. Larry's eyes kept searching the crowd for the face of a boyhood friend, John H. Rynearson. Finally he asked Rockhill. "I don't know where he is, Lawrence," said Rockhill, "but I know he got caught coming out the back window of the hardware store after closing hours and did time in prison a few years ago. He's in Mentone, someplace."

Rynearson had become the town scandal. No one in Mentone would have anything to do with him, but he refused to move away. Although he was respected as a willing and capable workman, he had become a depressed, periodic drinker.

"Say, where's my good friend, John Rynearson?" Larry asked those around him as he walked through a display of Bell-Sarber family relics, including Larry's cradle, his fishing pole, and countless clippings and photographs concerning Bell

Aircraft accomplishments. But there was no answer to Larry's question. No one wanted to ruin the day by having Larry see what had happened to his friend.

Bell never insisted but merely asked about Rynearson occasionally as the day progressed. Finally, the strategy worked. He heard a whisper and instinctively looked around. There in the crowd stood his old friend in a pair of dirty trousers and a rumpled shirt with no tie. Larry shuddered. What he saw was all too familiar: Derelicts on Buffalo's lower Main Street stared with Rynearson's same frightened, lost expression. Rynearson had wandered to the fair tent from the town's only restaurant, which had hired him for the day to wash dishes.

Larry walked swiftly to his friend and gave him a hearty greeting. Rynearson flushed with embarrassment and seemed to shrink away, so Larry put his arm around his shoulder. "Let's get out of here and get some lemonade," said Bell.

Alone at the refreshment stand, the two men talked over old times. Gradually, a crowd gathered. ". . . and, John," said Bell in a booming voice, "do you know you taught me the greatest lesson in contract negotiations that I ever learned?"

"Who, me?" asked Rynearson.

"Yes. Let me remind you," said Larry. "Remember the time I had a pile of firewood to split and pile, and I got you to help me?"

Rynearson shrugged.

"I bet you my brand new 8 cents worth of fishing tackle that I could pile the wood faster than you could split it. And when we started, you chopped so fast I didn't dare go near the axe.

"'Say, John,' I told you, 'This isn't fair. You've got to toss the wood out where I can get at it without losing an arm!'

"You said that was okay, and we started again. But then you chopped a piece and tossed it as far as you could in one direction, then tossed the next piece as far as you could in another direction.

"'Now they're out where you can get 'em, Larry Bell!'" you yelled as I ran back and forth.

"I was whipped, and I lost my tackle. But I learned a lesson in negotiations: When you make an agreement with a man, it isn't enough to say what he shall do and what you shall do. You've got to say what he shall do and what he shall *not* do."

Rynearson smiled. "Yes, I remember."

John Henry Rynearson never left Mentone. He committed

suicide three years later and was buried, without a headstone, in the cemetery where Larry's brother Edmund and sisters Blanch and Ethel are buried. Bell visited the graveyard later and asked to see Rynearson's stone. When he was told there had been no money to buy a monument, he murmured, "To hell with that." He told Rockhill, and they arranged to have an appropriate monument installed.

"It was a grand idea," Rockhill wrote, sending Larry the bill after paying half himself, "and it took you to remember the unmarked grave. I want you to let me share in carrying the idea through. You are still the same Lawrence, who never seems to forget; that is one of the admirable traits which you have and one of the characteristics that makes you one of the outstanding industrialists in America."

As the company prospered following World War II, Larry established the Bell Foundation, a charitable trust run by Bell Aircraft executives and dedicated to providing funds for a wide range of scholarships and causes. When the Bell Foundation sponsored a new library for the Mentone School, Larry returned home for the dedication ceremony on the night of April 20, 1955. It was one of the warmest get-togethers of all for Bell and his home town.

Rockhill made welcoming remarks recalling that Larry's grandfather, Christian Sarber, was one of the early settlers in Indiana, receiving a land grant in the township on April 10, 1843. He also recalled a favorite Bell saying, "Pretty good is *not* good," and advised young listeners in the audience that they also could find success by striving for perfection. "Lawrence did the best he could with what he had," said Rockhill.

The crippled attorney noted that Larry insisted on special consideration to employment for the handicapped. (When the work force had reached a total of eleven thousand persons on the Niagara Frontier, sixteen hundred of them were disabled persons.) "Their attitude is wonderful, and their attendance record is high above our factory average," said Larry. In the back of Larry's mind when he saw a handicapped person was Morrison Rockhill, who had been crippled for life and frequently was in great pain. Despite his physical problems, Rockhill had become a prominent lawyer.

In Buffalo on July 9, 1955, Larry finally was able to get together with some of the men and women who had helped him start the company in 1935. Of the fifty-six original employes,

The Bells visit Indiana for Mentone's "Larry Bell Day" during the war. Morrison Rockhill and Larry are standing. Seated, from left, are Lucille Bell, Harriet Morrison, and Harriet's mother Isabel. The photo was taken at Rockhills' home in Warsaw, Indiana.

'Go Wash Your Face, We Can Expect Mr. Bell Anytime!'

twenty-one were still with the company. They shared filet mignon on flaming swords and other delicacies at the Park Lane with the founder that night.

Ray Whitman was master of ceremonies, and Roger Lewis, assistant secretary of the air force, gave Bell the Exceptional Service Award, the highest honor the air force could give to a civilian. "As one of that small band of American pioneers who have conspicuously contributed to the development of air power, the name of Lawrence D. Bell is characterized by indefatigable efforts to assure America's continued air superiority," said Lewis.

The Department of Defense had announced earlier that year Bell Aircraft's role in the U.S. Army Nike anti-aircraft guided missile program. Bell built rocket engines for this missile, which was installed in hundreds of strategic locations throughout the country. One battery was placed on the road behind the Niagara Falls plant.

Larry achieved a personal goal in late 1955 when his Society for the Rehabilitation of the Facially Disfigured established a Clinic for Reconstructive Plastic Surgery of the Face. The clinic was built in the Manhattan Eye, Ear, and Throat Hospital, 210 East 64th Street, New York. Using funds provided by Larry's society, the clinic was set up with special equipment for treating everything from cleft lip to major disfigurement, such as that suffered by Jacqueline Auriol. Larry announced the program would "treat facial disfigurements as well as the psycho-social and vocational problems associated with the facially disfigured; the funding of fellowships and residencies; promotion of research projects and the supporting of teaching clinics." Dr. Converse was surgeon-director, and Dr. Harry H. Shapiro was executive director.

Larry's own health was failing rapidly. He was under the constant care of his heart specialist and Bell plant physician, Dr. Carroll Keating, and spent an increasing amount of time in the hospital. For years he had been suffering from coronary artery disease and a general hardening of the arteries. On May 24, 1956, Larry suffered a severe stroke that left him temporarily blinded. He recovered his sight, but the end was near.

His health kept him in Buffalo when the residents of Hurst and Euless, Texas, decided to name a high school in his honor. Despite the importance Larry placed on such honors, he was unable to attend the preliminary ceremonies. The event brought to mind another place named for him, and while still bedridden Larry inserted a $10,000 bequest for Larry Bell Park, Marietta, Georgia.

It was lonely in Larry's private hospital room. He looked small, sitting in bed, and his eyes moved restlessly toward the door whenever there were footsteps outside. Several books were on the bedstand, but only one looked as if it had been disturbed. A half-empty bottle of scotch rested in a shoe box in a corner of the closet. In a coat pocket was a rosary given to him by a little Chinese girl in Taiwan a few years before.

"Carroll," Larry asked Dr. Keating, "are you telling people to stay away from here? Where the hell are all my friends?" Dr. Keating was making notes in the medical record and looked up to see if Larry was serious. The utterly defenseless look in the suffering man's eyes made the doctor look away. There was no answer to the question.

One new acquaintance became a frequent visitor in Bell's last months. The minister of the Delaware Avenue Baptist Church, Robert Zearfoss, spent long hours with Larry, listening to stories from the days with Grover, Lincoln Beachey, and Glenn Martin. As always, Larry's memory was sharp. He wove countless details into each episode, and sometimes at the height of a story he'd wipe his eyes filled with tears of delight.

On September 18, Larry resigned as president and was elected chairman of the board. Leston Faneuf succeeded him as president. Larry was hospitalized again in less than a month. He was stricken with a heart attack on October 10 and battled ten days before succumbing to congestive heart failure at 5:10 P.M. on Saturday, October 20, 1956, in his sixty second year.

Lawrence Dale Bell left no family other than the 20,500 employees of his company. Everyone seemed to recall a personal moment with Larry, and countless memories were exchanged in the plants and offices. Lucille and friends from times gone by returned to Buffalo for the funeral from the downtown Baptist Church and burial in Forest Lawn Cemetery.

"You always knew he was here," said a white-haired second shift sweeper at the Niagara Falls plant. "It just seemed he'd be wandering this place forever."

Bibliography

Caidin, Martin. *Barnstorming*. New York: Duell, Sloan and Pierce, 1965.

Donovan, Frank. *The Early Eagles*. New York: Dodd, Mead, 1962.

Everest, Frank K. Jr. and John Guenther. *Fastest Man Alive*. New York: E. P. Dutton, 1958.

Friedlander, Mark P. Jr. *Higher, Faster and Farther*. New York: William Morrow, 1973.

Foulois, Benjamin D. and Col. C. V. Glines. *From the Wright Brothers to the Astronauts*. New York: McGraw-Hill, 1968.

Gauvreau, Emile, and Lester Cohen. *Billy Mitchell*. New York: E. P. Dutton, 1942.

Gibbs-Smith, Charles H. *The Aeroplane: An Historical Survey*. London: Her Majesty's Stationery Office, 1960.

Jane's All the World's Aircraft. London: Jane's Yearbooks, 1913–1956.

Macmillan, Norman. *Great Flights*. New York: St. Martin's Press, 1965.

Mason, Herbert M. *Bold Men, Far Horizons*. Philadelphia: J. B. Lippincott, 1966.

Roseberry, C. R. *Glenn Curtiss: Pioneer of Flight*. New York: Doubleday, 1972.

Shister, Joseph, and William Hamovitch. *Conflict and Stability in Labor Relations; A Case Study*. Buffalo: University of Buffalo, 1952.

Wagner, William. *Reuben Fleet and the Story of Consolidated Aircraft*. Fallbrook, Calif.: Aero Publishers, 1976.

Whitehouse, Arch. *The Early Birds*. New York: Doubleday, 1965.

Articles

Boyne, Walt. "Sky Tiger." *Airpower*, Sept. 1971, pp. 20–37, 62–66.

Miller, Jay. "Mach 3.0." *Wings*, Part I, Jan. 1976, pp. 40–51; Part II, Feb. 1976, pp. 46–53.

Neal, Ronald D. "The Bell XP-59A Airacomet," *Journal of the American Aviation Historical Society*, Fall, 1966, pp. 155–78.

Sinclair, Frederic. "The Daring Young Men in the Flying Machine." *True*, Nov. 1956, pp. 44–45, 56, 62.

Speech

Faneuf, Leston. "Lawrence D. Bell: A Man and his Company." An address before the Newcomen Society in North America, May 15, 1958.

Index

257